WILD + FREE
NATURE

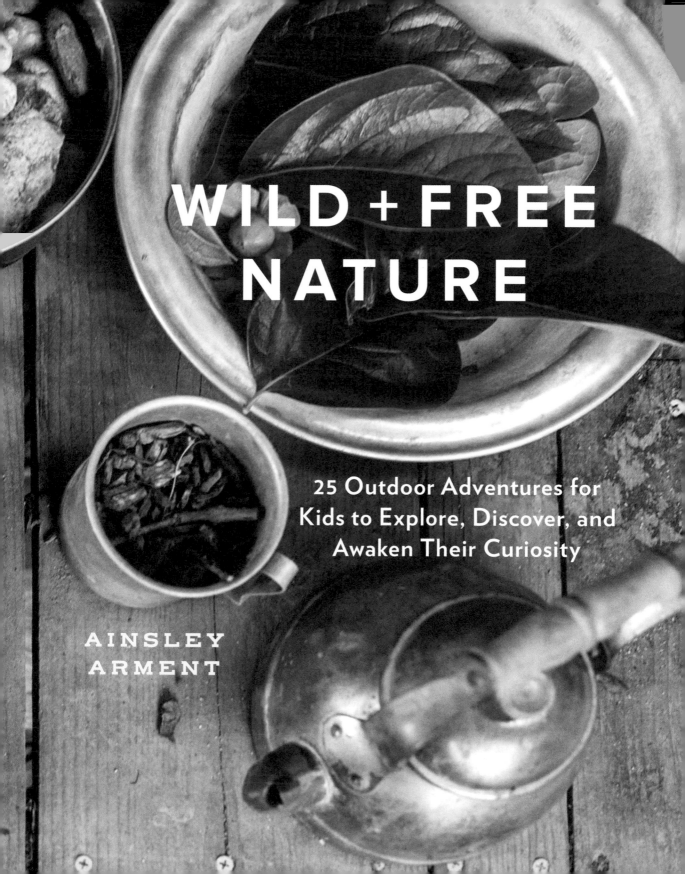

WILD + FREE NATURE

25 Outdoor Adventures for Kids to Explore, Discover, and Awaken Their Curiosity

AINSLEY ARMENT

HarperCollins books may be purchased for educational, business, or sales promotional use. For information, please email the Special Markets Department at SPsales@harpercollins.com.

FIRST EDITION

Design adapted by Elina Cohen
from the series design by Janet Evans-Scanlon

The chapter "Painting with Nature" was previously published as "Nature Paintbrushes" in *Wild + Free Handcrafts.*

Library of Congress Cataloging-in-Publication Data has been applied for.

ISBN 978-0-06-291657-0

21 22 23 24 25   TC   10 9 8 7 6 5 4 3 2 1

"Go out, go out I beg of you
And taste the beauty of the wild.
Behold the miracle of the earth
With all the wonder of a child."

—EDNA JAQUES

CONTENTS

The Wonder of Nature by Ainsley Arment   ix

THE WONDER OF NATURE

I grew up in West Point, New York, a tight-knit military community nestled along the grassy western bank of the Hudson River. For a few memorable years, home for me was a modest townhouse with a small side yard and a wooded hill across the back alley.

I was a strongly introverted child, and nature brought me tremendous peace and comfort. When ordinary life was too much, I went outdoors and found a friend in solitude. In the wild, life made sense to me.

It was up on the hill behind my house among the spruce and fir trees that I figured out who I was. When I was alone—no matter that civilization was just a stone's throw away—sitting atop a giant rock perched on the sloping landscape, I discovered a safe space where I could think, dream, and simply be.

As I look back over my life, I realize that I have always felt most at home when I am a little lost—in the wilderness, in the crowd, and in my thoughts.

I've seen it with my own kids too. They light up when they are bounding down the trail or making their own path through the trees. They delight in discovering a bug they've never seen before or spotting a majestic bird perched high in the trees. They're captivated watching a thunderstorm roll across the sky and splashing in rain puddles with their bare feet.

Even the ones who don't get quite so excited about exploring nature seem to come alive after spending time outdoors.

John Muir once wrote, "Everybody needs beauty as well as bread, places to play in and pray in, where nature may heal and give strength to body and soul."

If we are going to restore the wonder of childhood, we must give our children abundant time in nature. If we expect our children to one day care for the Earth, we must help our children fall in love with their planet. If we want to help our children become wild and free, we must give them a childhood steeped in nature.

Time in nature is not a luxury. It is a necessity. And we must give our children time to explore, discover, and get to know the world, which brings endless delights and lessons that never cease.

Whether you are a mama who needs to rediscover the power of nature or one who already chases down every adventure, this book is for you. I hope these stories, lessons, and tutorials give you permission to fall in love with nature again. I hope this collection is a magical portal leading you back to the forest, mountain, and sea. I hope it beckons you home.

AINSLEY ARMENT
Editor | @ainsl3y

WANDER

The word *wander* gets a bad rap. For many, it infers a lack of foresight, responsibility, and discipline. Wandering is something you do when you don't have a goal or purpose in life. We certainly couldn't live an intentional life or teach our children to become responsible adults if we regularly carved out time to simply wander, could we?

But wandering can have profound benefits for our souls when we think of it in a new light. J. R. R. Tolkien's observation that "not all those who wander are lost," applies to journeys of all kinds, not just those of hobbits. Wandering can have intention and purpose, and you will always get something unexpected out of it. That's the beauty of it.

We need permission to rediscover the wonder in learning. I want to give you permission to wander.

Wander into the woods.
Wander into the city.
Wander into fields. Wander to the sea.
Wander on a ferryboat.
Wander on a bike ride.
Wander on a whim. Wander on a farm.
Wander from routine. Wander
from curriculum.
Wander from safety. Wander
from boredom.
Wander far away. Wander close to home.
Wander to get lost. Wander to be found.
Wander into adventure.
Wander into the yonder.
Wander into the wild. And
wander into wonder.

WANDERING
CLOSE
TO HOME

remember the exact moment I knew I would marry my husband. We had only been together for a few months, and we were visiting my hometown, where he would be meeting my family for the first time. We went to a bookstore, and I picked up a book of travel photography. As I flipped through each stunning image, I told him of the places I'd always dreamed of going someday.

He put his arm around me and said, so sincerely, "I want to go to all of those places with you."

Eleven years have passed, and we're parents of four. We still hold our travel dreams closely, but only a few of them have come to pass, due to the financial and logistical realities of having four babies in our twenties. We look forward to many future travel experiences, with our kids and as a couple, but in the meantime we've learned to find adventure right where we are.

When we travel, we love to experience both the culture of a place and the natural areas surrounding it. We visit shops, museums, and hiking trails, walking through both cities and forests. Cultivating a sense of adventure without actually traveling is as easy as seeking out the places someone would visit if they were traveling to your own local area.

Here are some ideas for making the most of wandering around your own hometown.

NATURE NEARBY

Pull up a map and look for beaches, trails, parks, and other outdoor areas you've not visited that are within a two-hour drive. Pack a picnic, bring a book or a football, and make a day out of exploring this new spot together. Doing this has given us a much deeper appreciation for the features of our local ecosystems and the unique beauty of the area where we live.

HOMETOWN HISTORY

Every place has a story of origin. Diving into local history has been such an interesting learning experience for us. Look for historic stories set as close to home as possible, and visit historic sites such as battlefields, ruins, monuments, and museums. Before the trip, go to your library or local bookstore and find some books written for young readers that bring the history to life. Your children will be so excited on the trip, pointing out the spots they read about!

Knowing how your local area fits into the bigger stories brings history to life for you and your kids.

SHOP (AND SIP) LOCALLY

One family outing we enjoy is to go downtown, visit our favorite coffee shop, and then ride the free trolley. It's amazing to see how much fun the kids have with such a simple excursion. We also enjoy spending a morning at the green market, trying a new locally owned restaurant, or browsing a shop full of items made by local artists. Your whole family will feel more connected to your local community.

CULTURE IS EVERYWHERE

Find out what's happening culturally in your area, and explore ways to be part of it. Locate your nearest art museums. Go to plays, concerts, or dance performances. Some theaters offer daytime showings and special rates for families and school groups. One town near ours hosts a sidewalk painting festival every year. Another frequently has live music outdoors once a week, in a downtown courtyard. Public libraries often have calendars full of wonderful events.

WHEREVER WE GO, I try to encourage my children to be interested in what's around them—to notice things and be curious about them. I consider this kind of immersion in our local area to be very good practice for future travel. It allows our entire family to get used to seeking out new experiences wherever we are. It makes us more aware of the potential and richness of any place we might find ourselves, even when that place is our own backyard.

BY HANNAH MAYO

FORAGING IN NATURE

This past year, our homeschool nature group had the privilege of meeting up with a professional forager, Scott Nelson, who taught us about stinging nettle. Have you ever been playing in a field or walking near a steam and suddenly felt a painful sting? You most likely brushed up against stinging nettle. Here are some interesting facts we learned, followed by a tutorial on painting stinging nettle with your kids.

IDENTIFYING STINGING NETTLE

Stinging nettle is identified primarily by its location, shape, and color. All the senses are used in foraging, including smell and touch, but a forager usually begins by looking at where the plant is growing and what shape and color its leaves and stem are. Stinging nettle likes to grow very close to water—not necessarily in the water like watercress or monkey flower, but right next to it. You will usually find it growing along creeks in the wild, though you may also find it in places where the soil holds moisture or is regularly watered.

Stinging nettle is usually dark green and sometimes reddish and has jagged teeth along the edges of the leaves, which are opposite and ovate. The stem looks as if it is covered in tiny hairs. It can grow quite tall, up to several feet, and has little seeds at the tip of the stem when it is mature.

OUCH, THAT STINGS!

The plant is not poisonous—it just stings. Only the stem stings because it is covered with tiny needle-like hairs that are filled with a variety of compounds that cause the stinging. The best remedy is aloe vera gel or juice to sooth the sting until it goes away.

WHAT ARE ITS USES?

Stinging nettle, which grows in the spring, is used primarily to make a healthy tea called a *spring tonic*. In herbal medicine, a tonic is something that strengthens your body's systems. Stinging nettle tea has a unique flavor and is good for your kidneys, gastrointestinal tract, and urinary tract. The leaves can also be eaten as greens and are high in protein. Throughout history, the fibers in the stems have been used to make clothing and rope. Some people say that the sting from the nettles is a good treatment for arthritis, but maybe that's just because it hurts so much that you don't feel anything else!

MAKING YOUR OWN SPRING TONIC

It's easiest to harvest the plant with gloves and a pair of garden shears. Clip the plant above the ground, and place it in a bag. It may be used fresh or dried for later use. Simply place the whole plant or just the leaves in a pot of boiling water for five minutes or so. Strain the tea and drink as often as you'd like.

FORAGING AT HOME

Find a foraging book that is written specifically for your area. Then take the book on walks to try to identify the plants. In the interests of safety, Scott cautions against eating what you find. If you are interested in foraging for edible food, do so with an expert who can show you what will be safe to bring home and consume. You can bring a few plants home, as long as they are not endangered or protected by law. Whenever possible, take just a few of the leaves instead of pulling up the whole plant. Study all of the plants' characteristics, and then try to identify them without the book.

 SAFETY TIP

Be sure the plant hasn't been exposed to pesticides and hasn't been collected from a roadside. Consuming dried or cooked stinging nettle is generally safe. Do not eat if pregnant or expecting to become pregnant.

MATERIALS

Pencil with eraser

Drawing paper

Water

Palette

Watercolor paint

Paintbrushes

Micron pen 005

INSTRUCTIONS

1. With a pencil, lightly sketch the outline of your plant. For proper representation, make sure the leaves are opposite each other on the stem and have toothed edges. To make your painting more interesting, include some leaves that are folded.

2. Add a bit of water to your palette, and begin mixing the lightest shade of green that you see on your plant. Once you get the desired shade, take your wet brush to dry paper and begin placing the color where you see it on the plant. Use a smaller brush for the small leaves, stem, and snug areas, and switch over to a bigger brush for the larger leaves.

3. If you begin to add your next shade of green to your paper before the previous color dries, the paint will shift and move and blend together with the other layers. I love doing this, but at times I want a more controlled and pigmented look, so I wait for the bottom layer to dry before I add my next layer. Choose the look you desire, and begin layering the different shades of green. Be sure to notice if the underside of a leaf is lighter or darker than the top, and paint accordingly.

NOTE: When I want a deep green, I add dark brown slowly into my green shade until I get the desired darkness.

4. Once all your shading is done, let it dry completely.

5. Use a Micron pen to add an outline where desired. My lines are never complete or perfectly traced from beginning to end. Use the pen loosely and imperfectly for a more natural look. Don't forget to add all the tiny hairs on the stem!

BY KRISTIN ROGERS

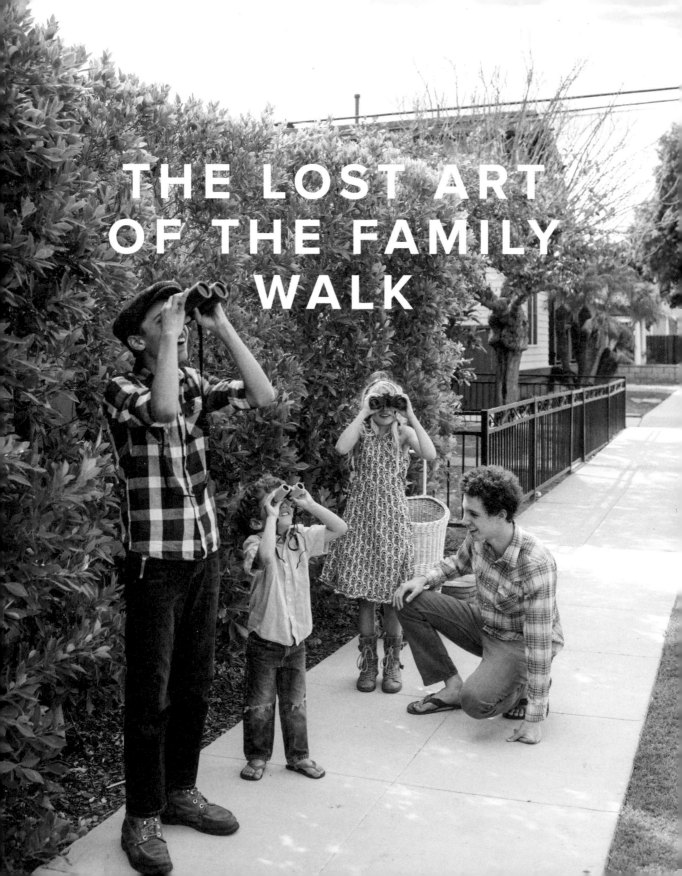

THE LOST ART OF THE FAMILY WALK

As a family that loves to travel, we realized that one of the reasons we love being in new places together is because of the hours we spend on foot—exploring, being surprised by what's around the corner, noticing the architecture, and taking in all the details. And those are all things we can experience in our own town. A family walk is unstructured time, an opportunity to get some fresh air and be free of electronics.

Our favorite route is a serpentine path of undeveloped land that used to be a part of the old Pacific Electric trolley line in California. Today, it is a habitat for native California plants. We take this path when we go to our favorite swimming spot—the lagoon. Walking through these neighborhoods, we see old craftsman-style houses and California bungalows. We like to notice the details: porches, columns, and unique colors.

And we will usually take a longer route home because any walk is better if it involves ice cream. We head to a tiny market that sits in a residential neighborhood—the store is a cute, dark-wood structure with umbrella-covered seating out front—and we each get an ice cream bar from the freezer case.

I'm amazed at how often we appreciate the landscapes and cities that are far from home but tend not to notice the beauty around us or visit the sites in our own town that a tourist would stop to see. The thought occurred to me as I was reading the book *French Kids Eat Everything* and learned about a charming Christmas tradition in the author's small town in Brittany, France. On Christmas morning, the residents walk with their children down the cobblestone path to the port to meet a boat that is decorated with lights. A sailor hands out gifts to the waiting children.

I found myself thinking about how wonderful it would be to grow up in a town with such a unique tradition. And then I realized that this experience isn't all that different from my own city's Christmas boat parade, which I sometimes go to but rarely appreciate as I should. And we have never walked to it, even though it would not be a terribly long walk. This year, we plan to walk to our local boat parade.

Some cities and towns are built for walking, while other places are more difficult to navigate on foot. They may be more spread out, or the traffic may discourage walking. But quite often, it is our own outlook that makes going for a walk a rarity. We are in a hurry, and our schedules are full. Slowing down enough to walk to a destination causes one to reflect and wonder, rather than just operate out of routine.

Since we started walking to more places, we have found new places to add to our list. We've been walking to our favorite coffee shop for a long time. But now we also walk to a bakery, our farmer's market, local shops, and a few parks. What once seemed like a distance too far to walk now seems like an enjoyable outing. The more we walk, the shorter those distances become to us.

There are many things I enjoy more if I walk to them. Driving to the farmer's

market for a few items seems like a hassle at times, especially when I think about loading the children into the car and finding parking. But walking in the fresh air makes me see the outing as a full experience, and that is more valuable to me than just getting the items I need. It's like stepping back in time.

TAKE YOUR FAMILY FOR A WALK

Think about some destinations within a mile or so from your home: Is there a park in your neighborhood? A place with specialty coffees or a boutique restaurant? How about an ice cream shop? Is there a market or farm stand within walking distance?

Use that as your destination, and take the scenic route.

Or walk without any destination in mind, and look at the houses and trees in your neighborhood. Whether you have a destination or not, it's fun to engage your kids with questions about what you're seeing:

- Can they point out any similarities or differences in the architecture of the homes?

- Can they identify any of the local flowers, trees, or bushes?

- Do they hear any birds or see any squirrels darting past?

- If they could live in any of these houses, which one would it be, and why?

- Can they make up an interactive story about something they see on your walk?

BY JENNIFER DEES

SAVORING WINTER

For most of us, it is a joy to be outside with our children. We take them outdoors when we need to get things done, we walk on trails with them, and we sit under a towering tree to read or to nature journal.

Then the rough months hit. For those in the south, it's the blazing hot summers. But for those of us in the north, it's the freezing temperatures of winter that challenge our nature-loving ways. Still, one year, I was determined to get my children outside more often in the winter months.

I found that I actually enjoyed winter more than I had in previous years. It was cold and long (snowing at the end of April), but because I had spent time outdoors, I was able to appreciate the beauty winter offered. I was able to push beyond my struggles and experience the virtue of winter alongside my kids.

If you are determined to get outside more and enjoy the spectacular and unique beauty that winter brings, here are some ideas that helped my family.

PROPER CLOTHING

We have slowly been acquiring quality winter gear. I paid a friend to knit hats for my girls. I researched the best boots. The children all have coats and snow pants that keep them warm. And I have begun investing in wool. Proper clothing can be an investment, but I have found that it is worth the money if you want to help your children (and yourself) enjoy the cold temperatures.

COMMUNITY

Not only is it more enjoyable to be out in nature with friends, but it also provides accountability that is crucial on days when you don't feel like bundling up all the children. You could find a local Wild + Free group that takes nature walks in the winter, or you could invite a neighbor or close friend to spend time with you outside. Find community in whatever way works for you, and enjoy the brisk beauty of winter together!

ATTITUDE

Last year, when I was determined to enjoy winter, I found that I really did, and my children did as well. Sometimes I had to will myself to look for the beauty, but over time it became more natural, and by the end of the season I could honestly say that I really had enjoyed the winter months.

RESPONSIBILITIES

We live on a farm, so we have animals that need to be fed whether it's rainy, sunny, or bitterly cold. This encouraged us to get outside because we had to! Some days, I preferred to run out on my own and do the chores, rather than bundle *all* my little ones up, but I tried to be diligent in making it a family activity. If you don't live on a farm, you can find other responsibilities to get you outside. Take out the trash, walk the dog, pick up sticks, fill the bird feeder, or maybe just walk to the mailbox together.

SIGHTS TO SEE

Find a path that you love, and walk it often, so you become familiar with it. Or choose a particular area of your backyard. Visit the same tree, creek, den, or bird feeder as often as you can throughout the winter, so it becomes known to you and gives you purpose as you head outside in the cold.

BY ALISHA MILLER

GROWING
INTO A
NATURE
MAMA

I did not grow up eagerly exploring the outdoors that surrounded our country home. The closest my family got to camping was when my dad pitched a tent in the backyard right under my parents' bedroom window. This way, my mom could talk to us from the comfort of her bed while my siblings and I spent the night under the stars with my dad.

It's taken time for me to become a nature mama. So, how did I get to the point where I crave time outdoors?

For starters, I've had to work at growing this desire in me. I long for my kids to have a childhood where they remember getting dirty, muddy, and wet. But I've had to learn how not to hover over my children as they climb trees and explore the streams near our home. I've also learned to be *happy* when my kids show up with dirty pants and muddy shoes. But the more I learn to enjoy nature myself, the more my kids fall in love with it as well. Here are some tips that have helped me.

KEEP A NATURE JOURNAL WITH YOUR CHILDREN

Starting a nature journal helped me notice nature and increased my desire to learn more. I enjoy incorporating nature journaling as part of my morning reading time before the kids wake up, and I often paint with them during our schooltime.

Start by taking notice of what is happening right outside your window. Is there a woodpecker? Blossoming trees? A line of ants heading to an anthill? Then get your colored pencils, markers, or even watercolors, and write or illustrate what you see. My kids and I once journaled as a goose laid her eggs a few feet away in a neighbor's gazebo. We noted when she laid the eggs and were excited to see the baby goslings emerge when they hatched.

Other ideas are to journal about trips you've taken, birds in the yard, nature you've read about, and even pets.

EXPLORE NATURE *WITH* YOUR KIDS

The next time your kids go outside to play, try going with them. My tendency is to send my kids out in nature and enjoy the quiet space inside to complete my own agenda. But I've seen how much joy it brings them (and me) when I go out with them from time to time and take part in nature with them. For instance, my son built his own fort in the woods last month and was excited to explain all of its features to me. See what your kids have to show you outside!

FIND A NATURE BUDDY

One thing that has helped me grow is having friends who enjoy the outdoors.

My friend Kristen approached me about starting a Wild + Free nature group in our area. When we sent word out that we were going to be starting a group, we had an overwhelming response.

Getting to know other nature lovers and going on outings together is a great way to drive your love for the outdoors. Start small by finding a friend or two and asking them to go on a hike with you. Or look for nature groups in your area, and join them for an outing.

READ NATURE-THEMED BOOKS

Reading is a great way to learn about nature, both the kind we see in our backyards and plants and animals that live on completely different continents.

My children and I recently read *My Side of the Mountain*, which is chock-full of nature-related themes and animals. With every page, we discussed a different bird that we hadn't heard of before or a new type of tree. We made journals to keep track of the different types of nature we were reading about. I kept reference books near us each time we sat down to read another chapter, knowing that at least one of the kids would ask to look something up.

Follow up your reading by taking a related daytrip—like a trip to a mountain range or even a zoo—to bring the nature you read about to life for your kids.

BECOMING A NATURE MAMA is a journey. This past winter, I sometimes preferred cuddling up in front of my fireplace with a book rather than hiking in the cold. But every time I chose a nature outing over the coziness of the indoors, I treasured those memories with my children. My kids are growing up learning what it's like to be dirty, muddy, and wet in the outdoors—and I've even enjoyed getting dirty, wet, and muddy too.

BY RENEE HUSTON

CAPTURE

Teaching our children is like a forest. It is an endless *wonderland* of magic and discovery. The possibilities are everywhere—a hiking path here, a bed of moss there, wildflowers to pick, rocks to turn over, and creeks to explore. Sometimes we lose the forest for the trees—the difficulties and challenges of day-to-day life raising kids—and it can be easy to lose our way.

These trees draw our focus away from the destination and force us to question every step in what we otherwise feel called to do. Eventually, the trees are all we see.

Before long, we lose our way.

Instead of marveling at the sights and sounds of the forest all around us, we stop moving altogether. We set up camp at the nearest tree. We doubt ourselves. Become isolated. Discouraged. We get caught up in a method, obsess over academics, or worry about whether we're supposed to be here at all.

We get stuck in survival mode.

To find our way again, we need vision. We need perspective to remember why we came here in the first place.

Vincent Van Gogh said, "If you truly love nature, you will find beauty everywhere."

May we step back and see the beauty of the forest again and not let one tree, or a thousand of them, convince us that we're lost and shouldn't be here.

May we never cease to notice the wonders, document our discoveries, or capture the moments that make this lifestyle so wonderful.

This is the forest. And you belong here.

NATURE
JOURNALING THE
MUSEUM

recently took my daughters to the Natural History Museum of Los Angeles County, which leaves us in awe of the world. I told the girls I'd leave time for them to nature journal something that stood out to them when we got home. The girls, led by their curiosity, weaved in and out of the rooms and exhibits. They squished their noses and palms to the glass and took in all they could, from dinosaurs to birds. After hours of oohs and aahs, we headed home to capture something in their journals.

Visit your local museum, and instruct your kids to find something they'd like to draw when they get home. One of the things we decided to draw was a giraffe, and I'm including the instructions if you'd like to draw your own giraffe. Or have your kids use their imaginations and draw whatever it was that caught their interest at the museum!

HOW TO DRAW A GIRAFFE

MATERIALS

Pencil

Eraser

Drawing paper

Ruler

Palette

Water

Watercolor paint

Paintbrushes

Micron pen 005

INSTRUCTIONS

1. Sketch the giraffe lightly in pencil so you can erase and redraw as needed. I made light dots on my blank paper so I could make sure my drawing followed those main points of body proportion on the giraffe. I erased the dots when I finished my sketch. You can also use a ruler to double-check other details, such as the space between

the eyes, the width of the neck as it grows thicker, and the distance between the ears.

2. Mix the lightest shade you see in the giraffe, and start painting the first layer of color. I used tan, yellow, brown, and white to create this base shade.

3. Layers, layers, layers! Continue to add darker browns where you see them. This is what creates highlight, shadows, and depth. If you want a more blended look, keep a good amount of water on your brush. If you want a more defined look, use less water on your brush. I like to use a mixture of both techniques. Layering takes time, but these details matter. Remember, it is okay to be imperfect and incomplete. It adds character and a personal touch.

4. Using the Micron pen, add some black outlining here and there to make your painting pop. Be sure not to overlook that small white dot in the eye—the catchlight. This one small detail can make or break the realistic look of an eye.

BY KRISTIN ROGERS

PAINTING WITH NATURE

Art has been a part of my identity since I was a little girl. When I was seven years old, a neighbor girl who was a few years older sketched a simple portrait for me. It was thrilling to see how a few lines of pencil on paper could form something so delightful. I copied that portrait and the other figure drawings she had shown me. I later took art classes and loaded my sketchbook with art, filled with joy and growing in self-esteem.

One day I found myself with a seven-year-old of my own seized with her own need to create. She began asking for paper, colored pencils, clay, beads, tape, string, and, of course, paint! This need resonated with the artist in me, and I wanted to say, "Yes!" But as the grown-up in charge of sweeping floors and rinsing paintbrushes, I would instead hear myself say with a sigh, "Another day," or "How about a movie?"

I wanted our home to be a place of creativity and inspiration for my children. That meant stepping out of my comfort zone and welcoming some mess into our space.

Last year, I decided to start saying yes to paint. Sometimes that would mean dropping everything to get out paint and paper; other times it meant intentionally scheduling an art session later in the week.

I rearranged the paint supplies for easy access, got long-sleeved smocks for everyone, and found some good washable paints. We didn't do it daily or even weekly, but our smocks and watercolor boards bear the marks of young artists, while our dining room table has become our family art studio.

As we have made time for painting, I have found a lot of satisfaction in combining art and nature. The beauty of natural colors and forms is both inspiring and therapeutic. One way to bring some nature and sensory fun into your painting sessions is by making your own paintbrushes. These paintbrushes can be used over and over or discarded for easy cleanup. We did our painting at our dining room table "studio," but this would also make a great outdoor activity for a group.

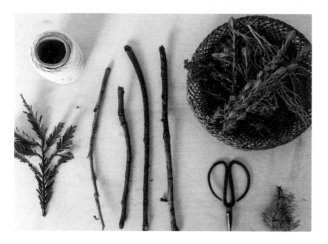

MATERIALS

String or rubber bands

Scissors

Bits of trees, grasses, or other plants for bristles

5 to 7 twigs for handles

Paint (I like washable tempura for this activity)

Paper

INSTRUCTIONS

1. Gather a variety of twigs, leaves, grasses, and other plants from outside. You can find what you need for this project at the park, your favorite nature spot, or even in your backyard. Evergreens such as redwood make nice sturdy brushes. We used herbs from our garden, which created nicely sized brushes of different textures.

2. Break twigs down into paintbrush-handle sizes.

3. Attach plants to the ends of the twigs using string or rubber bands.

4. Enjoy painting with the variety of brushes you have created.

BY RACHAEL ALSBURY

NATURE
JOURNALING
SQUIRRELS

My family loves all that nature has to offer, but it's sometimes difficult to transfer that love of nature to the page. But we discovered that keeping nature journals together is a great way to do so.

When I add a nature element to my journal, it's usually something I've encountered personally, something we discovered on a hike, a little creature that hangs around our property, or seasonal gems like fall leaves and berries. I encourage my kids to think along those lines, and it's always fun to see what they notice.

There is a whole family of eastern gray squirrels that lives in the blue spruce trees right outside my bedroom windows. Each morning, I see the mama jumping from branch to branch in search of food and supplies to bring back to her nest, which sits high in the fork of the pine branches. She was a perfect creature to include in my nature journal. If you'd like to try your hand at drawing a squirrel in your own journal, here's how.

MATERIALS

Pencil with eraser

Drawing paper or notebook

Watercolor pencils

Watercolor brushes

Gouache

Micron pen 005

INSTRUCTIONS

1. Always start with a line drawing using a regular pencil. This is where you choose the size and placement of your illustration. Where does it lie on the page, and why? Is it in motion? Does it need more white space on one side or the other? Will there be a background or not? I wanted to show my squirrel with some character, so I drew her with one paw up and made sure to show the curvature of her tail, as that's how I see her communicate with her family.

2. Once you have the lines where you want them, lay down the first color by dipping your paintbrush into a small amount of water. This is going to be the background color. In my painting, I used a light gray to

begin with. When deciding where to start, choose one of the lighter colors to use for the overall shade of the animal.

3. After you've chosen your overall color, look for variation. The overall color of my squirrel is gray, but she has browns on her haunches and face, darker grays on her tail and neck, and even blacks in her fur. Layer those colors from lightest to darkest. This may take some time as you train your eye to look deeper, but as you do, you will start to give your animal dimension. You'll also want to pay attention to how the light is hitting the animal. This will affect your color.

4. Even though my squirrel's belly is white, her undersides are shaded by the top of her body. I like to add shadows as I'm working with color and increase their contrast little by little. This is a personal preference, but I like to see a big difference between my darkest darks and brightest whites.

5. Adding the highlights is probably my favorite part; this is where the illustration really comes to life. Do so by adding a little sparkle to the fur where the sunlight hits it just right. And look at her eye! Putting that catchlight in the eye makes all the difference.

6. To finalize the drawing, use a Micron pen to add an outline here and there. In my example, you can see where I enhanced the fur, brought more sharpness to the eye, and added more detail to the claws and whiskers. These finishing touches give more definition to the animal.

7. Once you've finished, make sure to dry your pencils with a paper towel to keep them in good condition.

BY HEIDI EITREIM

PLEIN
AIR
PAINTING
WITH
KIDS

Plein air painting is more than just painting outdoors. It is the attempt to see nature in the changing light of moving time and to capture that fleeting image with paint. Artists lug their heavy gear to outdoor locations not only to see the beauty of the natural world but also to paint under the unique lighting conditions that you can only experience outside.

When you paint outdoors, you need to keep your equipment minimal and portable. And you also need to paint more simply and quickly than when painting in a studio. Due to the movement of the clouds and changes of the position of the sun in the sky, plein air painting challenges you to quickly commit to a pattern of lights and darks and add details with the most economical brushstrokes. This often gives plein air paintings a fresher look than paintings done in a studio.

It is the changing nature of light that makes plein air painting difficult and also a good challenge for an artist. When you paint from a photograph, you are looking at something static and two-dimensional, and the composition decisions have already been made. When you set up your art supplies in nature, there is a lot of visual information in your view, leaving it to you to decide how much of the scene and how much detail you will put into your work.

Plein air painting has allowed me to combine my love of nature with my love of art. One of my teenage sons loves to paint with acrylics, so we devised a plan to try plein air painting at a pretty marina near our house. We both found it difficult trying to capture the many boats and moving clouds, but we also fell in love with painting in the early, quiet hours.

There are so many benefits of plein air painting: scouting new locations and getting outdoors in the fresh air, challenging yourself, seeing color in natural light, and learning about the way artists have painted throughout history, not to mention making memories outdoors together.

Claude Monet famously said, "I have never had a studio, and I do not understand shutting oneself up in a room. To draw, yes; to paint, no." And many artists today feel the same way. Here are some simple steps to follow.

1. Decide on a medium. Acrylics are less expensive than oil paints, and they dry faster, so they may be a good place to start.

2. Pack a portable painting kit. The primary colors—red, yellow, and blue—and white are essential. I always use a cool red, a warm red, a cool yellow, a warm yellow, a greenish blue, and a true blue.

3. Bring water as a solvent if you paint with acrylics, linseed oil or turpentine if you paint with oils.

4. Pack a palette, paper towels, brushes, and a painting surface of canvas, panel, or even cardboard. A painting smock is also helpful for all ages—but especially for younger children who could easily get messy.

5. An easel is not necessary but is certainly convenient.

BY JENNIFER DEES

WILDFLOWER
ADVENTURES

In a recent class on foraging, my kids and I were taught to become familiar with toxic plants in our area. My girls identified the very pretty but toxic poison hemlock, which has attractive, white flowers that grow in small upright clusters. They spotted the stems, which are marked with small purple spots. All parts of the flower are poisonous, so I was glad it was on their radar.

We also learned that wild lilac, when rubbed in your hands with water, suds up like soap. We learned that Scotch broom adds nitrogen to the soil, which heals the land, and that black mustard is edible. We came across a lot of black mustard on our recent walk as well as wild radish. Wildflowers make for a beautiful and engaging subject to study. Here are a few of my favorite resources on wildflowers:

- *National Audubon Society Field Guide to California* (book)

- *Wildflowers of Southern California: A Guide to Common Native Species* (waterproof fold-up pamphlet)

- Flower guides from a particular place I'm visiting, typically found in a visitor center. Wildflowers can be hard to identify, so getting a local guide can help.

Here are some of my favorite resources for drawing wildflowers:

- *Nature Anatomy* by Julia Rothman

- *Hello Nature* by Nina Chakrabarti

- *The Amateur Naturalist* by Gerald Durrell

- *Nature Drawing and Journaling* by John Muir Laws

A few ideas for displaying wildflowers in your home:

1. Certain wildflowers like lavender and black sage look beautiful in a vase freshly cut. When they dry out, you can dump the water and leave them in the vase or remove them, tie a piece of twine around the stems, and hang them upside down on your wall.

Labels on image: California Fuchsia, Mustard, Encelia, Scarlet pimpernel, May Night shade, Wild Radish, Milkweed

2. Flatten and dry your flowers in a flower press or heavy book. Remove them and hang them upside down with a simple piece of washi tape anywhere on your walls. We love to do this in our kitchen.

3. As soon as you get home from a hike, lay your wildflowers on a cookie sheet with a wet paper towel over the stems and put them in the fridge. This will keep them in great shape with no wilting.

BY KRISTIN ROGERS

NURTURE

When my eldest was a baby, we lived in a townhouse on the outskirts of Washington, DC. We didn't have a backyard—or any yard for that matter—but there was an old gnarled pear tree in a tiny, four-foot mound of dirt between our front door and the parking lot.

This humble tree housed nests of songbirds every spring, served as a shady canopy for our old brick row house in summer, turned a brilliant gold every autumn, and created a magical view out our window with each winter snowfall.

I have dozens of memories of that tree: listening to the birds as the morning light streamed through the leaves while I fed my son at our tiny table by the kitchen window, hanging lights on its branches at Christmastime, and watching my toddlers climb its exposed roots for a little domesticated adventure.

In many ways, the tree that grew outside my window helped me rediscover a love of nature, my childlike wonder, and the desire to raise children who were wild and free.

A few years ago, we found ourselves back in our old stomping grounds and decided to drive by the old house. The first thing I noticed—or rather didn't notice—when we pulled up to the house was the tree. It was gone.

As I sat in the parking lot, looking at the house we called home those four years, the memories of that old rickety tree came flooding back.

To be honest, I didn't spend much time in nature during my son's early childhood, aside from occasional walks on the neighborhood trails while wearing him against my chest or later playing with him at the park. But we had that tree.

As I allowed a few tears to fall at the sight of its absence, I smiled at the memories. I thanked that old tree for giving me a second chance.

To nurture a love of nature in our children, we must first nurture it within ourselves. We cannot raise wild and free children if we are not wild and free ourselves.

Wake up to watch the sunrise, and fill your lungs with fresh air.

Drink your morning coffee on the porch to the sound of birds.

Set a reminder to go outside to marvel at the full moon.

Lay a blanket in the backyard, and look for shapes in the clouds.

If you take time to nurture your soul in nature, you'll find yourself falling in love with it again.

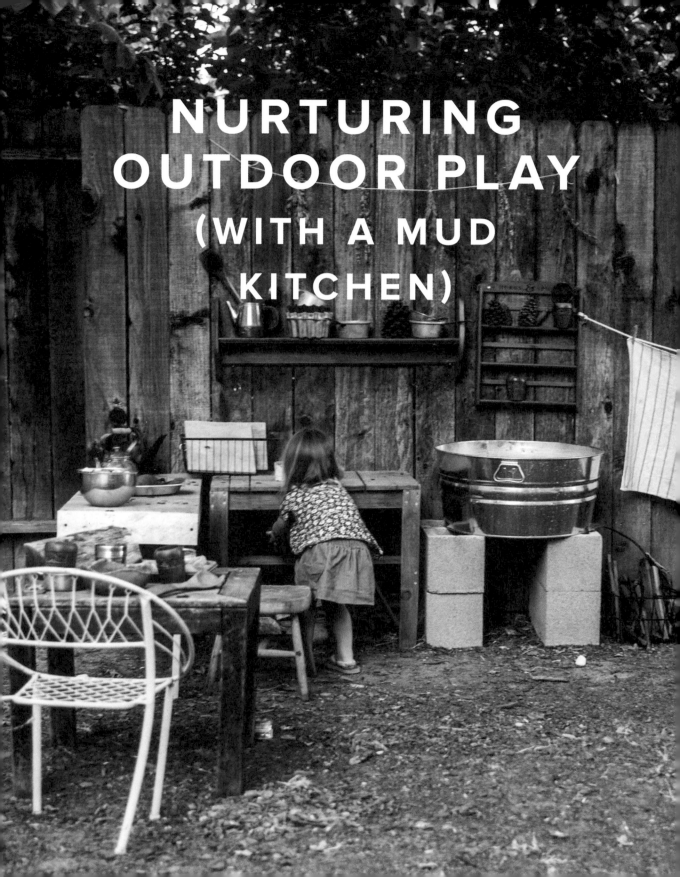

NURTURING OUTDOOR PLAY
(WITH A MUD KITCHEN)

One of the biggest challenges I've faced is getting my reluctant children to enjoy playing outside. I had visions of lightning bugs in Mason jars, long hours of survival play, and old-fashioned games like hopscotch and jump rope.

Instead, my girls shrieked at every bug they saw, refused to step foot off the patio, and wailed at the back door on perfect seventy-degree days. Our first hikes were not exactly the serene, sunset excursions I had envisioned!

I soon realized that one of my jobs as their teacher would be to show my girls how to enjoy spending time outside. With so many stimulating activities and devices competing for our attention, outdoor play was something I had to deliberately nurture in both myself and my children.

After about a year of consistency and intention, we emerged victorious. These days, you will find my girls outside almost daily, naming birds, holding ladybugs, and immersed in imaginative free play.

HELPING KIDS GROW COMFORTABLE OUTDOORS

My family committed to being outdoors for one to two hours a day (we live in a mild climate in Northern California). We spent time dealing with phobias surrounding dirt and bugs, and read piles of library books about ants, ladybugs, flowers, birds, and gardening.

Next, I found things we enjoyed doing in our own yard. We spruced up our mud kitchen (see instructions for creating your own on the next page) and put air in deflated bike tires. I stocked up on bubbles, sidewalk chalk, and bug-catching supplies. While the girls played, I joined them outside in my own sort of play: planting rosemary and lavender in my neglected flower beds.

I also went on a mission to find a nature spot that we could observe year-round. A nature spot does not have to be exotic or far away. In fact, our favorite local hiking place is located behind a suburban neighborhood. I like to make visiting our nature spot a special event by meeting friends, taking a picnic, or making it a family outing. These hikes often include a "nature hunt" where the girls gather treasures for our nature collection.

Another thing that helped was reducing overstimulating objects and activities. It is hard for the slow, meditative activity of being outdoors to compete with nonstop exposure to handheld devices, flashing imagery, and instant gratification. Purging excess toys and reducing our screen time for a season helped reawaken our senses and wean us from our dependence on technology for entertainment.

Like exercising and cooking nourishing meals, spending time outdoors often requires discipline. I get myself out the door, when I'd rather be in, by staying consistent and focusing on the benefits (such as having my children fall asleep quickly at bedtime).

HOW TO MAKE A MUD KITCHEN

Setting up a mud kitchen is a simple project that can go a long way in making your yard an attractive place for little ones to play. Our rambling mud kitchen is a mishmash of secondhand and repurposed pieces. We started with a simple table and some utensils and have slowly added on over the years. It has been everything from a cupcake shop to a "lost kids" hideout.

A hodgepodge setup gives children the ability to arrange and rearrange their space, while a more formal construction makes for a tidy, contained play area.

INSTRUCTIONS

1. PICK A SPOT. Pick an out-of-the-way location (preferably shaded) where you won't mind some untidiness. A non-landscaped area works wonderfully and gives children a space to dig. Along a fence is ideal for hanging pegs and shelves.

2. PROVIDE A STURDY WORK SURFACE. The work surfaces in our mud kitchen are built from scrap lumber and repurposed patio furniture. Stumps, thrifted furniture, old chairs, and boards laid over cinder blocks make great mud kitchen countertops. (Just make sure whatever you use is free of splinters, old nails, and sharp edges.)

3. FIND UTENSILS. Check garage sales and thrift stores for kettles, pans, cupcake tins, gelatin molds, wooden spoons, small cups, tin cans, and shakers. My children love to come along to the thrift store and shop for their kitchen.

4. ADD SHELVING AND STORAGE. Assembling some storage for displaying and rearranging utensils is half the fun of a mud kitchen. You can construct shelving from scrap lumber, pallets, or thrifted shelves. (Ours are both thrifted.) Wire baskets and buckets hold "firewood." Pots, pans, and cups can hang from hooks or pegs on a fence.

5. DECIDE ON A WATER SOURCE. Water play is an essential part of our kitchen. For a long time, we simply had a few containers for carrying water from an outdoor faucet. Recently, we added a "sink" made of a galvanized metal tub set atop some cinder blocks. (The tub is from the pet section of our home improvement store.) You can also add "running water" by using a plastic water dispenser. Some mud kitchen designs have a real sink or inset plastic tubs. Just be sure to supervise little ones around large containers of water.

6. INVITE PLAY. Fill vessels with fresh water, set out some "loose parts" (containers of pebbles, sticks, leaves, or acorns), hang herbs or flowers, and gather wood to make a "fire." A table and chairs, sandbox, play clothesline, or children's garden make fun additions. Hanging old sheets as a canopy over our kitchen is one of my favorite ways to set the scene for an enchanting afternoon of outdoor play.

BY RACHAEL ALSBURY

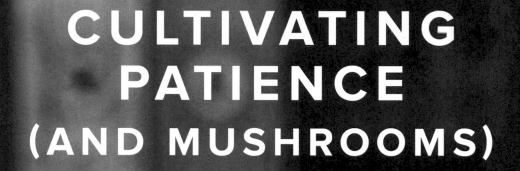

CULTIVATING PATIENCE
(AND MUSHROOMS)

Oh, end of winter, you seemingly never-ending abyss of darkness. The kids are moody, the skies are gray, and whenever we leave the house, it takes triple the time to go anywhere. Seasonal depression rolls in with the sub-zero wind chills.

At this point in the year, the only thing getting us through is the fantasy of early spring. Some years, winter is such a bleak, relentless season of deep burnout and impatience for me that it's nearly impossible to see the light.

So this year, I thought I would be clever. I'd chase down those pesky winter blues, and I would clobber them with productivity. I researched constructing a little indoor greenhouse, but as much as I was into it, I wasn't into the price tag. This led me down the internet rabbit hole of what was realistic and affordable that I could grow indoors in the winter.

And there it was, my winter salvation: We would grow mushrooms. On a log. In-

doors. Naively, I thought to myself, *How hard could it be?* Besides, if we could funnel some of our longing for springtime energy into a neat little project that made us feel like the thaw was coming, what could it hurt?

I adore mushrooms. They are beautiful, earthy, and fascinating. But when it came down to it, I didn't know much about growing them. It turns out that preinoculated logs are available from bigger stores like Terrain and Williams Sonoma, or you can go to a local farm stand or even unconventional places like Amazon and Etsy.

For this project, we wanted to explore different types of mushrooms, so we selected several different varieties from various sources. The phoenix oyster log was from Terrain, and the white-button and cremini/portobello boxes were from a local farm-to-table mushroom shop called River Valley Ranch (they ship if you are interested). And we got the morel spores from a shop on Etsy for a great deal. Each type of mushroom arrived promptly and required a different process to be successful.

This is where the patience comes in. The morels came with the simplest set of instructions: just soak the spores for twenty-four hours in unfiltered rain water, then dump them somewhere you find suitable for growth in your yard. Easy. Except for the part where it would take six months for morels to even think about appearing. Cue unjust disappointment.

That's okay though, I had the log! It came with a detailed instruction sheet that had several steps to get us where we needed to be, but there it was at the bottom of step 4: "Soak log every six weeks until the log is ready to fruit at four months." *Four months.* In four months, we would be in the midst of spring, smiling and feeling the sun on our faces every chance we could. That couldn't possibly help us now.

I felt my heart beginning to sink. Finally came the white-button and cremini/portobello boxes, which would produce mushrooms with some love and proper care within a month. A month was doable. We set to work, and the boxes were both a hit with the kids and a fruitful success! Let me offer you the insight that the month has offered me.

This project, waiting for mushrooms to grow, put me in touch with one of the things I struggle most with, and pulled me out of my rut by making me face something that I couldn't even see—my own impatience with winter.

While I won't find myself celebrating the snow, I will find myself trying to be more patient with winter, as well as more aware and even more forgiving. It's cold and messy and disorganized from time to time, but this life is still my passion. Patience is key.

My mushroom-growing month has taught me this very simple fact. Everything will grow in a few months. Maybe, just maybe, it's okay to rest in the meantime.

BY SUZI KERN

MUSHROOM PRINT ACTIVITY

Making a spore print from a mushroom is beautiful and fascinating, and the color of the print helps with mushroom identification. This is an easy project that can be done with mushrooms from the grocery store.

Here's how to do it:

1. Choose two mushrooms and cut off the stems.

2. Put one mushroom cap on a light piece of paper, and the other on a dark piece of paper, which will give two different prints.

3. Cover the mushrooms with a glass cup or bowl.

4. Leave alone overnight. In the morning, lift the bowls and mushroom caps, and you will have amazing spore prints!

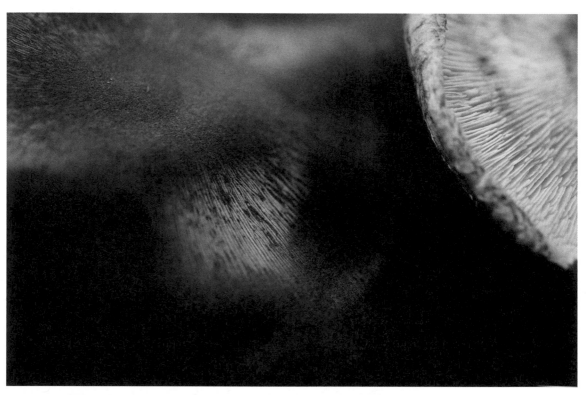

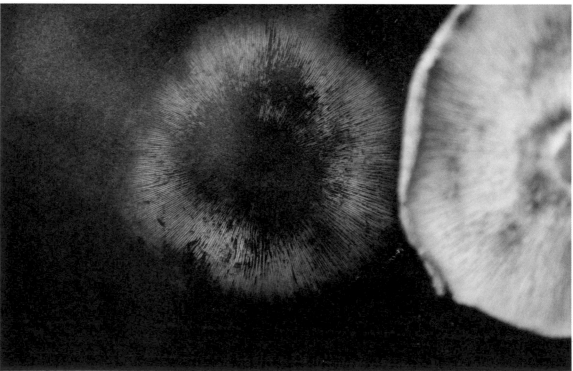

RESOURCES

A Field Guide to Edible Mushrooms of California by Daniel Winkler

This is a thin, foldable book with vibrant pictures and a guide to show which mushrooms are edible. The author identifies each mushroom as "choice," "good," "caution," or "poisonous/deadly." I'm excited to add this small resource to my nature bag for the occasion when I actually come across a mushroom in California.

Katya's Book of Mushrooms by Katya Arnold and Sam Swope

This is a wonderful children's book about Katya's life growing up in Russia and hunting mushrooms. The illustrations are cute, and it has both narrative and scientific aspects to enjoy.

The Magic of Mushrooms (television documentary)

If you watch this, I guarantee you will be in awe of mushrooms.

The Mushroom Book: How to Identify, Gather, and Cook Wild Mushrooms and Other Fungi by Thomas Laessoe, Anna Del Conte, and Gary Lincoff

This book has beautiful photography and is an informative guide!

The Mushroom Fan Club by Elise Gravel

This is a darling children's book written and illustrated by a mother of four who is fascinated with mushrooms. This book offers great information about mushrooms in the sweetest way possible. My girls loved it!

Nature Drawing and Journaling by John Muir Laws

I use this book all the time because it has specific drawing tips for mushrooms.

BY KRISTIN ROGERS

KEEPING CHICKENS

We have owned chickens for about ten years now. We learned so much along the way about how to care for them, help them thrive, treat illnesses, learn their habits, and appreciate the fact that they are so much more than egg layers.

Besides fresh eggs for breakfast, one of my favorite things about chickens is their humor. We crack up at the way they run, sway their necks, hug, and come quickly when they hear their name, and how their wattles move. They are so strange, cuddly, and fun. Through the years, we have even let our ladies wear a "hen holster" (chicken diaper) and hang out in our house.

If you're considering getting some chickens of your own, let me share with you what we've learned over the years.

Many people purchase chickens from a hatchery online. Some hatch them at home with an incubator. We purchased our chicks from a local feed store. We know that chickens do not like to be alone, so we always purchased at least two birds, but a minimum of three is highly recommended.

Pullets are what females are called during their first year of life. After that, they are called *hens*. *Cockerels* are what male chickens are called for the first year. After that, *roosters*. You do not need a rooster for your hen to produce eggs; you only need a rooster if you want to get fertilized eggs and hatch more chicks at home. Once a rooster and hen mate, her eggs will be fertilized for up to four weeks. Over the next couple of weeks, the hen will lay eight to twelve eggs, a *clutch,* and begin to sit on them. Although a hen's eggs and waste leave her body through the same "vent," the hen turns her cloaca and the last section of her oviduct inside out so the egg emerges far outside and does not touch the areas of her vent that touch her waste. This is why eggs are clean when freshly laid.

Once the eggs are warm, they begin growing. At this point, the hen will rarely leave her nest, keeping the eggs warm and rotating them regularly. A hen that sits on eggs with the hopes of them hatching is called *broody*.

The incubation process takes twenty-one days. Inside each egg is everything the chick needs to grow. By day 3, the heart is pumping blood that carries water and food from the yolk to the growing chick. By day 10, the wings, legs, and beak are fully grown. By day 14, the chick has grown a bump on the end of its beak called the *egg tooth* that will assist in hatching. On day 20, it will peck a hole into the pocket of air at the end of the egg to breathe for the first time. And on day 21, it will begin to hatch.

The chick can take up to twenty-four hours to fully hatch. There is a lot of pecking and napping going on. It's very hard work for a chick to hatch. The egg tooth used to peck during hatching will fall off after a few days. Let the chick do its pecking work with this tool. Interfering with the hatching process can harm the chick.

Once the feathers have dried, you'll have an incredibly cute, fluffy, and cheeping chick. These little guys are like the ones

we have bought in the feed store. Isn't that fascinating? They just went through that twenty-one-day journey and are ready to be cared for by their mother or in a brooder (a heated container that houses the chicks) by their new family.

Once the chicks are about six weeks old, they are ready to go outside in their coop. You'll need to wait another five to six months for them to start laying their first eggs. The larger the breed, the longer the wait. Different breeds have different egg productions as well. Each of our Rhode Island Reds gives us six eggs a week!

On average, a hen lays 260 eggs a year. After her first two years of life, her laying will begin to lessen and then eventually stop completely. This is when many farmers will turn them into chicken stew, but our hens become our pets and live out the rest of their lives in our backyard.

With proper care, chickens live five to eight years. They can die earlier due to illness or predators, and I have read of some chickens living over fifteen years, but that seems pretty rare. Can you imagine all of

the studying you and your family can do over the years of caring for a flock? You can study their behavior, eating habits, feathers, and social interactions with one another. I hope to dig deeper into many of these topics myself as we continue our chicken adventures.

BY KRISTIN ROGERS

NURTURING SLOW IN THE CITY

My family lives in California in a medium-size city. Our neighborhood is quiet and feels like a small town at times, but the areas surrounding us are anything but. We have to drive thirty to forty minutes for true quiet and wild nature. I love where I live, and I love the coastal experiences we enjoy, but I often find myself yearning for a place that is slower and sleepier.

Every place has its own set of challenges and benefits. I find that if you live in a large town or a big city, it takes a lot of planning to live at a slow pace. My family has worked at nurturing a slow lifestyle in our city.

Here are some ways to nurture a slower lifestyle with your family.

- **CHOOSE BOOKS OVER SCREENS.** All activities are not equally restful and restorative. Reading will make you feel more rested, so opt for quiet evenings with books.

- **INSTITUTE A HOBBY NIGHT.** In my house, everyone picks his or her own book to read, art project to work on, or instrument to play.

- **TAKE EVENING WALKS AS A FAMILY.** The evening walk is our new favorite pastime and adds to our sense of slowing down and enjoying the details. It is a simple joy.

- **TAKE THE SCENIC ROUTE.** Even when driving to the store or to run other errands, I have often been taking the long way to my destinations lately. I drive through smaller streets and pay attention to the character of the different neighborhoods.

- **GARDEN.** We don't have a large yard, but that hasn't stopped us from having a large garden. Our city offers community garden plots, and this gives us adequate space to grow enough tomatoes to feed an army. The time we spend in the soil growing things is everything that my *Farmer Boy*–loving soul could dream of: quiet, purposeful, restorative.

- **MAKE TIME FOR CONVERSATION.**
I am learning to not hurry when I really don't need to. Getting to know your neighbors and the people who work in stores you regularly visit encourages conversation over rush.

As we think through the things that support a slower lifestyle and bring peace to our families, it becomes easier and easier to identify the activities that truly matter. Wherever you live, you can seek to be deeply invested in people and a few hobbies, rather than being caught up with a little of everything. Slowing down means I'm available for deeper relationships with my kids, spouse, friends, and neighbors. It has been helpful for me to remember that when life feels too hurried, maybe *I* am the one who needs to stop rushing.

BY JENNIFER DEES

EDIBLE FLOWER
AND HERB
COOKIES

Edible flower and herb cookies are beautiful and a fun project to work on as a family. They make teatime special and also make a lovely gift. We have used the petals of dianthuses, violas, and pansies. We have also made some cookies with sage and mint leaves that we harvested from our home garden.

A few tips before you make your cookies:

1. Use only flowers that you can identify and know are safe to eat, as some flowers are toxic. Make sure you know which parts of the flower are edible. Petals are usually used, as other parts of the flower are often bitter. If you are unsure if your flowers are edible, you can do a quick Google search to find a reputable source to be sure they are indeed edible.

2. Avoid flowers that have been treated with pesticides or chemicals.

3. Never harvest flowers growing by the roadside.

4. If you don't have your own organic edible flowers growing, you can purchase organic flowers at farmer's markets, from the produce section of your grocery store, or online.

5. Gently wash your flowers in a bowl of cold water and allow them to air dry on a paper towel before baking.

SHORTBREAD COOKIES

1 cup (2 sticks) unsalted butter, softened

½ cup sugar

½ teaspoon vanilla extract

2 cups all-purpose flour

¼ teaspoon baking powder

½ teaspoon salt

2 tablespoons milk

1. In a mixing bowl, beat the softened butter for about 30 seconds with an electric mixer at medium speed. Add the sugar and vanilla extract. Beat on medium speed until fluffy, about 1 minute.

2. In a separate bowl, whisk together the flour, baking powder, and salt. With the mixer on low speed, gradually add the flour mixture to the butter mixture, beating until just combined. Add the milk, and beat on low until just combined.

3. Divide the dough into two equal parts, and use your hands to form each part into a flattened ball. Wrap in plastic wrap and refrigerate for 1 hour. It is essential to chill the dough, as it needs to be cold for ease of cutting.

4. Preheat the oven to 350°F.

5. Remove the chilled dough from the refrigerator. Sprinkle your work surface, the top of the dough, and your rolling pin with a bit of flour, and roll the dough to slightly thicker than ⅛ inch. Alternatively, roll the dough between two sheets of parchment paper to prevent sticking.

6. Use a cookie cutter to cut the dough into cookies. With a small spatula, carefully transfer the cookies to a baking sheet. Re-roll the remaining dough scraps, and continue to cut out cookies until all the dough is used. If the dough becomes too warm as you are rolling it out, it may need to be chilled again.

7. Bake the cookies for 10 to 12 minutes, until the edges just start to turn pale golden brown. Allow them to cool on the baking sheet for 5 minutes, then transfer to a wire rack to cool completely.

LEMON GLAZE

1 cup powdered sugar

3 tablespoons freshly squeezed
lemon juice

Zest of 1 lemon

Edible flower petals or herbs

1. In a mixing bowl, whisk together the powdered sugar, lemon juice, and lemon zest until smooth.

2. Once the cookies have completely cooled, spread or brush the lemon glaze over them.

3. Gently press the edible flower petals or herbs into the glaze.

4. Allow the cookies to sit until the glaze hardens, and enjoy!

BY NAOMI OVANDO

GATHER

When my husband, Ben, and I began raising our family in the suburbs of northern Virginia sixteen years ago, we found ourselves drawn to the farmland surrounding our bustling town. On the weekends, we drove out to the countryside with our two toddlers to find secret creeks and stone-walled meadows.

As we've moved from place to place over the years, we've continued to seek out nearby parks, forests, and farms to allow our kids to experience the rural and rugged life as much as possible.

Richard Louv reminds us in *Last Child in the Woods* that it wasn't all that long ago, as recently as the 1950s, that most families still had some kind of agricultural connection. Children directed their energy in constructive ways: doing farm chores, raking hay, splashing in the swimming hole, and climbing trees. "Their unregimented day would have been steeped in nature."

Today we've industrialized our learning and homogenized our homes in concrete jungles. At a time when our lives are becoming more digitized by the day, our children need time to explore the natural world. They need contact with living things, fresh air in their lungs, and an understanding of what sustains them.

We can't all live on a farm or build a home in the middle of the forest. We can, however, still find places to experience the peace of the wild things, places that offer adventure, unregimented time in nature, and connection with your community.

Let's focus not on what we don't have but on what we do: nature walks in the neighborhood, hikes at the nearest national park, fishing at a nearby pond, and frequent visits to a favorite farm.

In her book *For the Children's Sake*, Susan Schaeffer Macaulay writes, "We all have limitations and problems. But I must never think of it as all or nothing. Perhaps I'd like to live in the country, but I don't. Well, maybe I can get the family to a park two times a week, and out to the country once every two weeks. Maybe I have to send my child to a not-so-good school. Well, maybe we can read one or two good books together aloud. If you can't give them everything, give them something."

Our children are gathering experiences and impressions in their proverbial gunnysacks of childhood. What we give them now are the things that will form their futures. What kinds of memories, moments, and mementos are they collecting?

That's it, then. If we can't give them everything, let's give them something.

THE NATURALIST AT HOME

Field observation is not the only way to enjoy nature—you can also bring nature home. Here are some ideas to consider as you build your collection.

SPACE

We live in a small home, so we carved out a small portion of a bookshelf for our collection and have a couple of specimens displayed on the wall. I know some families who keep their nature collections in a drawer so it is out of sight until needed. Think about a place in your home where you could keep a collection: a shelf, a drawer, a basket, or a closet?

DISPLAY

Display your nature collection in jars, shadow boxes, or shallow cardboard boxes with cotton. Items from your kitchen, such as empty jam or honey jars, are an inexpensive solution and create a beautiful learning environment.

You can create your own mini museum or simply carve out a small area to display your findings in a way that fits your home's decor. Using washi tape to display dried pressed flowers on a wall is a very simple way to show off your nature finds. Most naturalists recommend labeling and dating your specimens.

COLLECT

Our nature collection was gathered in the field or purchased. We collect feathers, rocks, acorns, shells, bones, nests, lizard skins, and so on. We built our collection slowly, and now that it's reached the desired size, we bring home only unique or special finds. Too large of a collection can feel like clutter and no longer be appreciated.

One time, we found an amazing insect display in a thrift shop. Upon reading the attached note cards, we learned it was a classroom project that students had created. We have also purchased a few collections and insect marbles off eBay. As

items break, chip, or fall apart, we replace them with new finds so that our collection remains tidy.

CLEAN

Make sure you check your collections to make sure there is no infestation. Look for holes in your specimens or fine dust or flaky bits underneath. It is best to destroy affected specimens. If they are too special to destroy, fumigate them.

USE

Not only does a nature collection create a wonderful learning environment but you can pull out your specimens and appreciate them over and over again. If it's a rainy day or the little ones are sick and you can't go out to the field, bring the field to them through your collections. Study them, write about them, and paint them in your nature journals.

BY KRISTIN ROGERS

A KITCHEN
SCRAP GARDEN

As a child, I remember planting seeds in tiny pots with my mother and anxiously checking them each morning to see if their tiny green heads had appeared. Days would go by until, finally, I glimpsed the pale green shoots. What a thrill to watch those tiny shoots grow! I remember my determination in digging hundreds of small holes outdoors to place them in, and I took such satisfaction in harvesting my hard work at summer's end.

Now that I have a family of my own, I want that same wonder, determination, and enchantment for my own children. But gardening is not possible in every living situation, nor is it feasible for every season of life. We have lived in apartments and have rented small homes with no yard space. We've tended large gardens, windowsill gardens, container gardens, and just "one small herb pot" gardens. The seasons of pregnancy required low-maintenance plants, while the energy of toddlerhood required resilient plants. Gardens can be expensive, especially if you don't already own the gear. And when children are involved, there is never a guaranteed yield.

That's where a kitchen scrap garden comes in. The beauty of a kitchen scrap garden is that you can do it anywhere, anytime. You don't need special equipment or a large space. It can be as large or small as you desire. You won't need to spend money on seeds; instead, you'll use some of your food scraps from the compost pile. Scrap gardens are incredibly kid-friendly and resilient, and they offer the perfect opportunity to discuss reducing food waste with our kids. It's a wonderful gift to use something we previously thought of as "garbage" to nourish, educate, and enchant our children.

Start small with one or two projects. And once your vegetables or herbs begin to take root and are ready for a pot, start another celery plant or jar of herbs. The kitchen waste bin can be your go-to throughout the year, and you'll have a variety of plants to choose from as summer returns and, with it, Earth's bounty. Your children will be able to see the same plants grow again and again, becoming attuned to the growth cycles of different plants. They will be able to monitor the growth of their plants daily, utilizing math skills while predicting when food will be ready to harvest. And they will gain further appreciation for their food, the work that goes into growing it, and the blessing of fresh fruits and vegetables.

MATERIALS

You'll need containers for the plantings, but here are tips that help save money:

- Find some inexpensive plastic pots at a secondhand store or online.

- Many times, you can find pots or gardening gear for free on the internet or at a local recycling center.

- Your local gardening center might have broken pots or plastic pots they no longer need.

- Save and use plastic containers you would normally recycle by punching a few holes in the bottom.

- You will also need soil for a few of the projects, so have some on hand.

INSTRUCTIONS

There are many options when it comes to a scrap garden. Here I've listed a few of my favorites, along with a description of how best to grow them and about how long they will take to harvest.

GREEN ONIONS OR LEEKS. Once you've used the green stems in your cooking, place the roots in a jar with water. You can wait until the root systems develop a bit and then transfer them to soil, or you can continue to let the plants grow in water, changing the water regularly. Trim the green part whenever you are in need of spice in the kitchen.

LETTUCE. Cut off the root end of the plant, and place it in a bowl of water, root end down, leafy side up. The plant should not be submerged. Place it by a window with full sun, and spray the top of the plant with water daily. Change the water every few days. In two weeks, the leaves should be long enough to harvest. Return the root to the water to sprout more leaves.

CELERY. Cut off the root end of the celery, and place it in a shallow bowl of water, stalk side up. Place it in a sunny area, and spray it with water daily. Change the water every

few days. In two weeks, sprouts will develop. After you see sprouts, it's time to transplant the celery to a pot of soil. Keep the soil moist. You can harvest the celery in several weeks and use it in your cooking! Begin the process again with your harvested celery plant.

HERB CUTTINGS. Basil, parsley, thyme, rosemary, sage, and lavender are great options for this technique. Clip a healthy-looking main stem of the herb plant. Place it in a small jar of water, making sure to trim any leaves that will be submerged. Change the water every few days, and keep an eye out for tiny roots. Plant the cutting in soil when the roots are about two inches long. Keep the plant in full or mostly full sun, and water well.

PINEAPPLE. Cut off the spiky part of the pineapple, making sure to remove all the yellow flesh, and place this core in a shallow bowl of water by a sunny window. Change the water every other day. Roots will take about two weeks to form, and when they reach one to two inches long, you can transplant your pineapple to a pot. New growth will emerge from the center, so watch carefully for the small green leaves to appear. Be sure to place your pineapple

outside during the summer to allow pollination. This creates a pineapple plant that can be kept all year round, provided there is a sunny window in your home. In two to three years, you could have your very own homegrown pineapple!

GARLIC. Separate a few cloves from the garlic head. Place some soil in a large container, then plant each clove about three inches deep and six inches apart. Water regularly, keeping the soil moist. Scapes (garlic shoots) will appear soon and can be trimmed and used for cooking. Regular trimming helps the garlic bulbs grow larger, so cut the plant down to the base regularly. When the green growth begins to turn brown and die, it is time to harvest. Hang the bulbs and allow them to dry for at least two weeks before using.

SWEET POTATOES. Set a whole, unpeeled sweet potato in a jar or glass of water, letting about half the potato be covered. When the water gets cloudy, change it. In a week or so, small nubs of roots will appear. Several weeks later, the potato will have developed a large root system and several tall green shoots. Trim the shoots off, and transfer them to a new jar of water. When the shoots have developed a healthy root

system, about two weeks, you can plant them in sandy soil to grow small sweet potatoes. When the shoots and flowers die is typically a good time to harvest the potatoes.

PEPPERS AND SQUASH. Harvest the seeds from a bell pepper, pumpkin, or any kind of squash. Place the seeds in homemade newspaper seedling pots or small starter pots about one inch deep, three seeds per hole, one hole per starter pot. Spray the pots with water, and place them in full sun. Water when the soil becomes dry. When the seedlings are three or more inches tall, they can safely be thinned and transplanted.

Keeping them in their starter pots, plant the seedlings into larger pots or outside in the ground in full sun. (Be aware of frost dates for your area, and don't plant outdoors until the danger of frost has passed.) Water regularly. If you plan to plant outdoors, be sure to harden your plants first.

LEMON. Harvest lemon seeds by cutting a lemon in half and scooping out the small seeds in the center. Do not use any seeds that have been cut. Put some soil in a pot, then plant the seeds one inch deep and two inches apart, one seed per hole, in as many holes as can fit in the pot. Spray with water and place in full sun. In one to two weeks, small sprouts should appear. Water when the soil is dry to the touch. When the seedlings get to be three inches tall, you can discard the weaker-looking plants and place each seedling you keep in a small pot. Regular watering is necessary, and the plants will need to be repotted as they grow larger. Lemon trees can grow several feet tall and will produce lemons in several years.

BY MOGLI LOFTUS

CREATING A BACKYARD HAVEN

For some time, I yearned to create a little haven in our backyard, which drove me to research our local flora and fauna and opened my eyes to the importance of creating a wildlife habitat in our Arkansas yard. What I learned is that in cities and suburbs across our country, the local flora has been stripped away and replaced with ornamental, non-native plants and trees. This process, unseen to most people, has impacted the local ecosystem.

Non-native plants do not provide the sustenance that the native animals need to survive, and so the animals move to where they are able to find food, often leading to their injury or relocation for pest or nuisance control. I have a dear friend who is a certified Master Gardener for our state, and she was more than happy to spend a little time teaching me about local plants. Many of the organizations we reached out to shared an abundance of information.

Interestingly, one of the best practices for your yard in the fall is to allow your leaves to remain on the ground. Leaf litter provides shelter for insects of all kinds, small reptiles, and amphibians, as well as foraging materials for the birds. This was easier said than done for us, as we live in a subdivision with expectations for yard upkeep, especially when considering the plethora of large oak trees on our property that drop leaves well into the winter.

And so we came up with a plan. Our front yard would be kept leaf-free, and we would place the leaves we gathered in our larger side yard and leave them as a natural compost pile of sorts. That leaf pile became home to some of the strangest beetles this past summer. I never identified them, but I hope to next summer if they return.

A log pile slowly transformed into a living wall—a haven for crawling things, mosses, and small plants. We had the great pleasure of seeing an array of mushrooms sprout up the following spring. Geckos, green anoles, skinks, and a small snake or two roam our little haven. One spring day, my children shouted to me that they had found a weird bug, and outside I raced.

It was a weird bug indeed. It took me a bit to figure it out. It was a wheel bug—one of the strangest insects I have ever laid eyes on—just slowly making its way across our back deck. A member of the assassin bug family, it is truly the most "metal" of all the insects; a large and dangerous-looking spiked wheel protrudes from its thorax. During our nature journal work later that day, our conversation focused on the rarity of what we had seen, and I couldn't help but wonder if our efforts to renature our yard were the reason the strange insect crossed our path.

Bird hotels, bat houses, and a squirrel home have all found a space in our backyard, constructed by my husband and children. The process of building those shelters is a delightful lesson for our entire family and a wonderful opportunity for my husband to have one-on-one time with each of our children.

Over time, the first bird hotel succumbed to the elements. Our second birdhouse was taken over by a darling squirrel. Watching its face peek out of the hole was such a joy. Unfortunately, our mighty hunter puppy caught the poor thing one day, and it was no more. This spring, I saw another squirrel move in, and once again I had the pleasure of a little squirrel face peeking out at me every once in a while.

MAKE YOUR BACKYARD INTO A WILDLIFE HABITAT

- For a small fee, the National Wildlife Federation will designate your yard as a Certified Wildlife Habitat. The process is quite simple and asks that you look at your yard for the following qualifications: food, water, shelter, a place for animals to raise their young, and sustainable practices. My children had a wonderful time reading through the checklist with me and making their own lists of what was missing in our little sanctuary. When your habitat is certified, you will receive a beautiful sign to place in your yard, the wildlife magazine, and other small benefits. Visit www.nwf.org/Garden -for-Wildlife.

- Start watching for the insects, critters, birds, and wildlife to take up residence in your backyard haven. Keep a log or

journal of the types of wildlife you see, and research them with your kids.

This process of building a natural haven in our backyard is ongoing. It requires a slow and steady tuning of our attention to the life all around us—a facet of life that we had once been oblivious to. Our focus on creating our own home has often come at the cost of the shelter of our nearest neighbors in the natural world. It does not have to be this way. You can transform your yard or garden, or even a small patch of sidewalk, into a small haven for some plant or creature. In doing so, you may just find that you cultivated a deeper sense of peace and place for your own shelter.

BY NICHOLE HOLZE

HEIRLOOM SEED EXCHANGE

Seed exchanges are created to facilitate the sharing of both seeds and knowledge. After visiting our local seed exchange, I left knowing that we had to start one of our own. My children and I did our homework and decided what type of exchange we wanted to create, and then we got to work. Here's what we learned about starting and participating in a seed exchange.

GETTING STARTED

What kind of seed exchange do you want to facilitate, and how would you like to execute it? We chose heirloom seeds and wanted to exchange them both locally and via mail with our friends.

Heirloom is a word that seems to get thrown around quite a bit these days, but what we discovered is that the main defining qualities of heirloom seeds are that they are open-pollinated (they rely on natural pollination from insects or the wind), they are easily saved from season to season while remaining true to type, and

they come from seeds that are at least fifty years old.

The benefits of heirlooms are incredible, from producing great-tasting and high-nutrient vegetables to being the more economical choice, since they can be saved from one year's crop to plant again the next year.

If you're interested in acquiring some heirloom seeds of your own, they are available from online companies like Baker Creek Heirloom Seed Company and Seed Savers Exchange. But you can also visit local farms, nurseries, seed libraries, and conservatories to purchase heirloom seeds that are local and therefore adapted to your environment.

HOSTING YOUR OWN SEED EXCHANGE

Now that you've got your seeds, let's get down to the business of hosting your seed exchange. After collecting your seeds, you will only need to have a few items handy to make the whole thing come together:

plain seed packets (easily purchased on Amazon for a few dollars), markers, and tiny volunteers.

This is a fun activity to do with your kids. Show them how to mark each seed packet clearly with the common name and Latin name of the plant, the year of collection, the year the seeds were grown, and the location of growth. Feel free to throw in some fun facts about who grew the plant, along with any other tidbits you find useful. Younger kids can decorate the outside of the packet. Finally, fill the packet with your preserved seeds and voilà! When we were done, my kids enjoyed drawing and photographing their harvest.

BY SUZI KERN

FORAGING DANDELIONS IN YOUR BACKYARD

Growing up, I was taught that dandelions were bad. If you had a yard full of them, it meant you didn't care about your yard. If children blew on them in the wind, then their parents didn't care about their neighbors' yards. And they were definitely not really flowers—they were *weeds*.

In reality, dandelions are a versatile, tenacious, and beneficial plant. They help treat everything from cuts and bruises to poor digestion. They can grow in extreme environments where little nutrients are available. And they are an excellent food for pollinators, bees included.

Every single part of the dandelion is edible and packed with vitamins A, C, and B, potassium, calcium, iron, protein, and phosphorus. The greens, most tender in the spring, were seen by our ancestors as a way to stimulate the digestive system after a winter's hibernation. This bitter green leaf helps to break down food. Dandelion greens can be eaten raw, combined in a salad with other leafy greens, sautéed, or made into a tincture.

Dandelion heads are delicious when fried lightly in coconut oil, incorporated into baked goods like pancakes or muffins, eaten raw, or infused into syrup. The heads have a nutty flavor and act as a great garnish for nearly every meal. The roots of the dandelion are deep, which is excellent for holding together the soil in your yard, but they can also be a lovely addition to a stir-fry or soup. You can also use the roots—dried and then roasted—as a coffee substitute.

If you decide to forage your own dandelions, try them in the following recipes.

DANDELION SALAD

Harvest several cups of dandelion greens and a cup or so of dandelion heads. Combine the dandelion greens with a couple cups of other greens you enjoy, such as frisée, lettuce, kale, spinach, or chard; sprinkle with the yellow petals. Add a couple tablespoons of olive oil, as well as salt to taste, and toss. Serve as a delicious summer side salad.

DANDELION STIR-FRY

1 tablespoon coconut oil

½ medium onion, chopped

2 garlic cloves, chopped

1 teaspoon chopped fresh ginger

2 cups shiitake mushrooms, sliced

1 teaspoon smoked paprika

½ teaspoon Vietnamese cinnamon

2 cups dandelion greens

1 cup dandelion petals or whole heads

2 tablespoons tamari or soy sauce alternative

½ tablespoon lemon juice

Cooked rice or other grain, for serving

½ cup whole cashews, for serving

1. Heat the coconut oil in a skillet on medium heat. Add the onion and sauté until fragrant, then add the garlic, ginger, mushrooms, paprika, and cinnamon. Cook until browned, roughly 5 to 10 minutes.

2. Lower the heat, and add the dandelion greens and petals, tamari, and lemon juice. Cook until wilted, about 2 minutes.

3. Serve the stir-fry over the rice, and top with the cashews.

DANDELION
SOUP

1 ounce dried astragalus root

½ cup fresh dandelion root, thinly sliced

½ cup fresh burdock root, thinly sliced

1 tablespoon grated fresh ginger

1 tablespoon dulse (edible seaweed)

2 tablespoons high-quality olive oil

1 medium onion, chopped

1 to 2 cups sliced shiitake mushrooms

2 to 3 garlic cloves, minced

½ cup miso paste

NOTE: You can find ingredients like astragalus root, burdock root, and dulse (edible seaweed) at health food stores or online.

1. In a large saucepan, bring three quarts of water to a boil, then reduce to a simmer. Add the astragalus, dandelion, burdock, ginger, and dulse. Cover and simmer for 45 minutes. Strain, discarding the solids, and return the broth to the saucepan. Adjust the heat to low.

2. In a skillet over medium heat, heat the olive oil and sauté the onion and mushrooms until tender, 5 to 10 minutes. Add the garlic, and sauté for 2 minutes. Add the onion mixture to the broth, stir in the miso paste, and enjoy!

DANDELION SYRUP

50 to 75 dandelion heads, green parts removed

3 green apples, peeled, cored, and chopped

1 stalk of rhubarb, chopped

1 quart filtered water

1 tablespoon lemon juice

2½ cups raw cane sugar (or natural sugar substitute, like honey, agave, or maple syrup)

In a large pot combine the dandelion heads, apples, rhubarb, water, and lemon juice. Over medium heat, simmer for 30 minutes. Strain, discarding the solids, and return the liquid to the pot. Add the sugar and bring to a boil. Stir until thick. Allow the syrup to cool, and pour into glass jars.

 SAFETY TIP

Only ingest dandelions that you know have not been treated with pesticides. Do not forage for anything near major roadways, where plants may have absorbed fumes and toxins produced by vehicles.

BY MOGLI LOFTUS

EXPLORE

Mama, come quick!" a voice called from the backyard. I stepped outside, where my little girl was kneeling before a cluster of white dunce cap mushrooms. "Look," she whispered. "Aren't they cute?"

She clasped her hands under her chin and looked at me longingly while her happy mushrooms peeked out from the blades of grass. I agreed, saying, "They aren't good for us to eat, but they do make the perfect umbrellas for fairies, don't you think?" I told her she was lucky to spot them because once the sun came up and the dew dried, they would wither away in the heat.

Our children are natural-born explorers, constantly on the lookout for wonder, excitement, and adventure. Society numbs this desire over time, but it doesn't go away completely.

A few years ago, my husband and I headed out for a low-key excursion with the kids. We took our children to the park, like we used to do when the older boys were little. We sat on a bench drinking our coffee and solving the world's problems while our children played. They explored a natural rocky area near a pond filled with lily pads and bullfrogs, rather than the manufactured playground equipment. I was careful to make sure no signs forbade it, but the other parents murmured their displeasure and cast disapproving looks in our direction as they ushered their curious children back to the plastic jungle gym.

Since when did childhood become an indoor activity?

Since when did we have to manufacture the environments for childhood?

The call of the wild and free is the call of nature, beckoning us back into its wild places.

Let's take our children out to the rivers and forests, the mountains and oceans. Let's let them daydream for hours at a time. Let's let them experience boredom and in so doing give them a fertile seedbed for imagination, play, and wonder. Let's let them swim in the creeks, run in the fields, get dirty, stay up late to see the stars, and catch bullfrogs with their bare hands.

We must let them spread their wings and explore without interference. Let them chase butterflies, sunsets, and dreams. Let them build and climb, get dirty and wet. Let them feel what it's like to play in the rain or dance under a full moon. Let them be wild. Let them be free.

And remember, if you want to raise explorers of the wild, you have to be one yourself. Get outside. Get dirty. Start oohing and aahing. Start wondering and wandering again. Be afraid. Be adventurous. If you lead the way, I promise, before you know it, your children will be leading you.

NATURE STUDY
IN THE CITY

grew up in a pretty average neighborhood in southern Michigan. I didn't see much nature that was out of the ordinary, but I spent many hours exploring my neighborhood, collecting blue jay feathers and wild mulberries, and wandering the ravine near my house, armed with a forked stick for trapping snakes. I wanted to know what creatures lived near my home but didn't know how to find them.

My own children, by contrast, have seen more amazing moments in nature than I ever did, and we live in a fairly large city in Southern California. Living in a city has not kept us from learning about nature. We see a great variety of bird species and insects around us, and many curious animal habits play out right before us. And it's not because we travel very far, but because we know where to look. More importantly, my children know *how* to look.

Experiencing wonder in nature is all about being observant and having patience— patience to look under rocks, into the foliage of the trees, and through binoculars, even when you are sure you only have sparrows in your neighborhood. We have seen documentary-worthy moments because we return to the same places again and again, no more than fifteen miles from our house.

One time, we found a giant water bug in a creek. We researched it and discovered it's simply called "the giant water bug." We learned it eats fish, and so we took our giant water bug home and bought goldfish from the pet store to feed it. We have since found dragonfly nymphs and other aquatic insects in our local creeks.

Another time, we got into a learning frenzy about moths. I read *A Girl of the Limberlost*, a fictional story about a girl who catches and sells moth specimens. I started researching the moths mentioned in this story and found that many beautiful moths live in the US. I became obsessed with the idea of finding a polyphemus moth in the wild. These tan-colored moths with large eyespots in the middle of their hind wings are named after Polyphemus, the giant cyclops from Greek mythology who had a single large, round eye in the middle of his forehead. We learned about their food source and where they have been spotted locally. The next step was to build a moth trap with a black light, which we ran from an extension cord outside my bedroom window. We even took it camping. We never found a polyphemus moth, but we made many memories.

My love for birds started with some blackbirds sitting on a telephone wire in my neighborhood. At first, I was sure they were all black, but when I looked through my new binoculars, I could see a purplish, iridescent sheen to the color and many yellow spots on their feathers. What we thought were blackbirds were actually European starlings, brought to the United States in 1890.

And thus began my love for bird-watching. Since that time, we have learned to distinguish many different bird families and their habits—a necessary skill for identifying birds. We now know where blue herons nest in our area, and we see great horned owls not too far from our house. We have seen Bullock's orioles, western tanagers, downy woodpeckers, and Amer-

ican kestrels—all in our neighborhood. We rescued a baby crow that fell into our yard in a heavy windstorm and raised it until it fledged. This clever crow, named York, loved to steal my kids' LEGO pieces and stash them on our roof. York was the best pet we ever owned. We know where to go to watch ospreys catch fish and even where to find bald eagles in Southern California.

Wherever you live, you probably underestimate the amount of nature near you and over-romanticize the nature you can only see in pictures. It's easy to think that if we only lived somewhere else, we would spend more time in nature—somewhere with more open space, more water, more trees, more trails. But it's important and wonderful to learn about nature no matter where we live.

Here are a few ways you and your children can bring nature into your city experience.

1. If you have a yard, a balcony, or even a window box, take time to learn about and plant species that are native to your area, which will attract the birds and butterflies that live near you.

2. Go on nature hikes.

3. Visit nature centers and other wild spaces near your house.

4. Invest in a good pair of binoculars; you can easily miss animals without them. And be patient. It can take some time for animals to appear.

5. Set out bird feeders, different styles for different birds.

6. Start an insect collection. Pinning butter-flies is a fun hobby.

7. If you have even a small yard, consider raising chickens.

8. Build a bat house.

9. Start a seashell collection, and identify the various snails and other mollusks that make these shells their homes.

10. Explore riverbeds, even when there is no water.

11. Read an inspiring book on local natural habitats, and buy field guides about local plants and animals.

12. Keep a nature journal, and label the plants and animals you are studying.

BY JENNIFER DEES

EXPLORING THE NATIONAL PARKS

Over the past two years, our family has fallen in love with visiting the US National Parks, and recently our adventures took us to Bryce Canyon National Park. Located in southwestern Utah, this park will make you feel as if you stepped onto another planet—a planet made of sandstone walls that resemble tall castles and rock formations that look like otherworldly characters. As you walk along the rim of the park, the views seem unreal. It is a park of geological wonders that stir your imagination.

Visiting a national park has a number of benefits, and one is that the national parks offer endless scientific learning opportunities. We learned that Bryce Canyon is actually not a canyon, but a series of amphitheaters carved into the edge of Utah's Paunsaugunt Plateau. These amphitheaters hold the largest concentration of hoodoos found anywhere on Earth. Hoodoos are rock formations made of limestone that look like tall, thin, whimsical towers.

We also hiked along the serpentine Navajo and Queen's Garden Trails, which led us to the floor of an amphitheater. There was something to discover and explore around every bend of the trail. All three of my children were in wonder and awe as they wandered through the hoodoos and walked through the red rock tunnels and arches. We learned about the Paiute, and since returning home, we have been inspired to learn more about the history and culture of the Native American tribes that once lived in the national park areas we visited.

In addition to the amazing geological formations and their brilliant colors, Bryce Canyon is one of the best places in the nation for stargazing due to its pristine air and distance from sources of light pollution. The skies are so clear that you can see all the way to the Andromeda Galaxy, which is 2.5 million light-years away. We live in the city, and it is not very often that we get to see starlit skies. It was amazing to see how many stars were visible with our naked eyes as well as how many stars we were able to capture with our camera.

By visiting the parks, we can inspire our children to love and respect these beautiful public lands and to protect the historic and cultural sites that tell the full story of America.

HOW TO TURN NATIONAL PARK VISITS INTO LEARNING

1. SCIENCE. National parks have some of the most stunning landscapes in the country with a plethora of wildlife. Pair your trip with learning opportunities about the different ecosystems and wildlife specific to this area. Check out books about the animals you saw, or keep natural journals.

2. HISTORY. The parks are also home to historical trails and archaeological sites. By visiting Bryce, we learned a little about the Paiute Native Americans. You can learn more about the Native American tribes— their history and culture—that once lived in the national park areas, or any other history specific to the park you visit. The early history of the Earth itself can also be learned. This is a great opportunity to learn more at the library when you get home.

3. CONSERVATION. Visiting national parks makes you more aware of the importance of learning about conservation efforts and protecting the amazing biodiversity and endangered species in the parks. Teach children to have a love and respect for these beautiful public lands as well as to protect these historic and cultural sites that tell the full story of America. Together with your kids, consider making a donation to park conservation or a related cause, or find a nearby park where you can volunteer together.

BY NAOMI OVANDO

THE MAGIC OF FIELD TRIPS

Butterflies in the stomach, brown paper sack lunches, bus rides, and big city adventures—these are some of my most vivid memories of grade school field trips. Unfortunately, as joyous as they were, I don't think I could tell you a single thing I learned on them. So here's the task I embraced as an adult and an educator: to combine the magic of field trips with true learning for my kids.

For one particular trip, we decided to tackle one of the greatest museums in the country: the Field Museum in Chicago. I didn't print out a single field trip guide or scavenger hunt. I put away my highlighters and fun facts and decided to let the day make itself.

The kids completely took over, asked questions, led us around, and soaked up tidbits from imagery and signs. The museum layout guided us. The exhibits produced their own questions. And the staff was phenomenal at sparking interest. All of the tools we needed to make the day enriching were there from the moment we stepped foot into the museum.

We spent the following week drawing pictures and writing down the kids' favorite tidbits from the trip. They printed their favorite photos and told their grandparents new facts. It was amazing how much they had absorbed.

There is a time and place for assignments. In the museum, it would have been an added pressure, but afterward at home, the lessons allowed the children to relive the trip. The work didn't even seem like a chore to them because they had had such a good time.

PLANNING A FIELD TRIP

- Is there somewhere in your area that would make a good "field trip"? Maybe a local or national park, museum, historical site, farm, or factory tour?

- Plan for transportation, appropriate clothing, and food if needed, but

otherwise leave the day open for exploration and enjoyment. Watch your kids light up as they discover bugs, dinosaur bones, or conveyor belts carrying chocolates.

- Later in the week, incorporate related activities into your school work or playtime. Draw pictures of the things you saw, read books, or study unknown animals. Use your imagination to come up with other ideas! If you bring the experience to life for your kids, the magical field trip memories will stay with them for years.

BY SUZI KERN

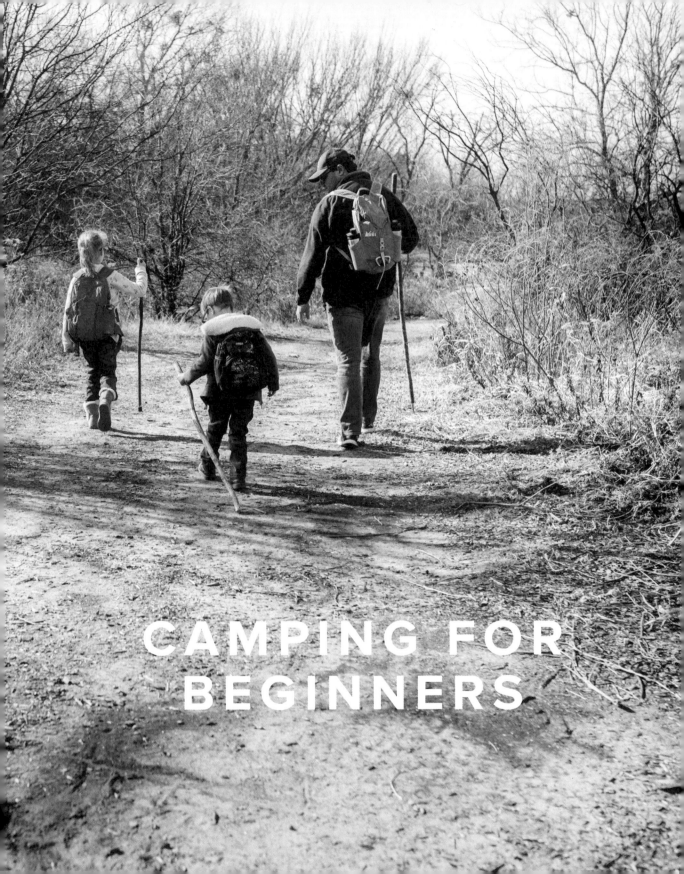

CAMPING FOR
BEGINNERS

did not go camping as a child, and so as an adult, I saw it more as work than as an enjoyable activity. My husband, however, along with his father and friends, had charted and traversed every inch of the government land near our home when he was growing up. His map-reading skills and survival instincts are on point. So when I agreed to do a camping trip with our kids, who were all under the age of four, I thought to myself, "Why on earth would we ever want to take them out into the wilderness in a tent?" My husband was adamant that this would be fun and that we would all enjoy the adventure. It was just one night in the national grasslands not far from our home. If things went awry, we could easily pack up and head home.

A study from Barry Garst, associate professor of youth development and leadership at Clemson University, found that children who grow up camping are more comfortable pushing boundaries in ways that improve self-confidence, strengthen social skills, and boost responsibility. I knew this was exactly what I wanted for

our children, but in order for that goal to be achieved, I had to start reaching outside my comfort zone and be willing to learn alongside them.

Since that time, I've learned many things about what makes a camping trip successful. If you, like me, lack camping experience but want to give it a try, here are some tips to make it go smoothly.

ASK FOR HELP

Whether you sleep in a tent or pack your family into an RV, there are always problems to be solved, but working together creates opportunities for cooperation and building one another up. Many people who love the great outdoors are thrilled to share their knowledge. We've found that simply asking for help can be the biggest boon to a trip.

Among our favorite resources are the local park rangers. I have yet to encounter a park ranger who seems rushed. Rangers have helped us find the best camping and hiking spots and have shared a plethora of tips for fire and general safety on the trails. They have even led us patiently on hikes well off the beaten path when one of my kids had a question.

THE MORE THE MERRIER

Camping with others who are more experienced is another great way to build your confidence. We regularly camp with several families. Not only have we all learned a ton from one another, but we have also built bonds that are strong and true.

We build upon ongoing stories that become more elaborate during each campfire circle and share a tradition of waking up together on Sunday mornings for breakfast in the woods. It is a time that our family has grown to cherish more than anything else.

Many scientists believe that these deep, ongoing social interactions help maintain good mental health. And there is no better way to become friends than to be out in nature away from all of life's distractions.

It's where you can really listen and really get to know the needs and heart's desires of your friends and their families.

ENRICH YOUR KIDS

Camping exposes children to a variety of scientific fields, such as botany, taxonomy, astronomy, ichthyology, entomology, and ornithology. You can even see chemical reactions at work when you allow your little ones to observe the wonders of fire building. We love nature journaling our experiences on the trails and in the camp and have watched our children emerge as leaders as they make new friends at the campground.

REDUCE STRESS

I notice a huge reduction in stress once we set up camp and begin to fully immerse ourselves in nature. I am able to engage more fully with my children and my spouse, simply because I have less on my plate. Our cell phones often refuse to work on camping trips, which is an added blessing for our time together. Scientifically, the increased oxygen levels experienced during time in nature provide your brain with greater levels of serotonin and controlled levels of mclatonin.

Over the last seven years, I have grown from a non-camper to a mom who is happy to hit the trails with her children, even when conditions are far from perfect. I owe all of this to taking that first step and admitting that I have to learn as I go—and that single lesson is one of the best I could ever teach my children.

BY BRIT CHAMBERS

FOREST
GAMES

Games are one of the oldest forms of human social interaction. They teach us, connect us, and provide a satisfying challenge for our physical and mental muscles. In a learning environment, they offer playful discovery in place of direct instruction. In a community context, they help us ease our way into new social interactions.

Here are some ideas for fun games that will connect you with nature and friends. There is something here to engage everyone: artists, naturalists, young athletes, and others.

LEAF MATCH

MATERIALS

An area with a variety of trees

A variety of leaves

Field guide (optional)

INSTRUCTIONS

The object of this game is to find the tree that matches the found leaf. Designate an area with a good variety of trees. (It helps to establish some boundaries with landmarks.) Mark off a smaller space for younger children and a larger space to challenge older ones. Have children wait outside the area while you collect an assortment of leaves.

Once you have a good sampling, have each child choose a leaf and go in search of the tree it belongs to. This game works best with a smaller group of children, so it is a good idea to split large groups up if needed. This is a great opportunity for naming trees. A field guide will come in handy for this one.

FOREST GUIDE

MATERIALS

A wooded area to play in

Bandannas or fabric to use as blindfolds

INSTRUCTIONS

This game is one part teamwork and another part sensory experience. Divide your group up into teams of two. One player wears the blindfold, while the other plays the role of forest guide.

Each guide chooses a special tree in the area. Their task is to carefully guide the blindfolded player to that tree. The guides must go slowly and help their partner avoid any obstacles in the path. As they are walking, they should also explain in detail what is along the route.

When they have reached the special tree, the guide helps their partner place their hands on the trunk and explore the tree using touch and smell. Encourage the guides to ask questions about the tree:

- Is the trunk big or small?

- What does the bark feel like?

- Does it smell like anything?
- Can you feel leaves or branches?
- Are there any roots sticking up from the ground?

The guides may also find a leaf from their tree to give their partner as an added clue. When the tree and its leaves have been examined, the guides take their partners back along the same route to the beginning point. The players then remove their blindfolds and use the information from their exploration to find the special tree. Once the tree has been found, the partners trade roles.

NATURE SYMMETRY CHALLENGE

MATERIALS

A wooded area with items like pine cones, leaves, and acorns

A flat area of either dirt or concrete on which to place your symmetrical design

Bags or baskets for collecting objects

INSTRUCTIONS

Split players into groups of two or three.

Explain the term *symmetry* (when one half of something is a mirror image of the other half). Point out that many things in nature are symmetrical. Have players go out and collect as many small nature treasures as they can find. Pine cones, acorns, and some leaves, feathers, and flowers are ideal examples of symmetry, but twigs and pebbles are also great comparison objects!

Once the natural elements are assembled, have the children organize them into piles of like things. Observe the symmetry (or lack of symmetry) in each. Draw a large circle on the ground. You can draw in the dirt or create a circle with pebbles, as we

did in our game. Have the first player in the group choose one element and arrange it symmetrically in the circle (see photo). The second and third players do the same until all of the objects have been used and the design is complete to everyone's satisfaction.

TREE TAG

MATERIALS

An area with room to run around

INSTRUCTIONS

Play a game of classic tag the forest way! Help children split into teams of "it" and "not it." It is helpful to designate some physical boundary lines for the play area.

You can vary this game by playing in an area with more trees (lots of bases to run between) or in a meadow with one designated tree base on either end. The winner of the game is the last "non it" player!

BY RACHAEL ALSBURY

CONTRIBUTORS

AINSLEY ARMENT is the founder of Wild + Free, host of the weekly *Wild + Free* podcast, and author of *The Call of the Wild + Free*, *Wild + Free Handcrafts*, and *Wild + Free Holidays*. She and her husband, Ben, are founders of the Wild + Free Farm Village and are raising their five children, Wyatt, Dylan, Cody, Annie, and Millie, in Virginia Beach, Virginia. | @ainsl3y

ALISHA MILLER is raising her own little women: four daughters, ages eight and under. Alisha follows the Charlotte Mason method and is thankful for the opportunity to give her children a beautiful and rich childhood. She also is thankful for the journey of life—a journey of learning, loving, and becoming. | @littlewomenfarmhouse

BEKAH MAKA is a part-time fitness instructor and part-time photographer who lives forty-five minutes from Washington, DC. She loves the beach and cold brew and will try any food once (unless it's labeled as spicy). | @bekahgracem

BRIT CHAMBERS and her family live in the mountains of Virginia at the Wild + Free Farm Village. They love exploring the land and charting all the new plants and animals they've encountered since moving from their tiny home in Texas. A mom through foster care and adoption, Brit is an avid advocate for orphan prevention. | @chasing.pure.simplicity

HANNAH MAYO lives in South Florida with her husband and four children. She is a writer and photographer who believes in the power of storytelling. She is also an online ESL teacher to students in China. She geeks out over theology, nutrition, film cameras, and fantasy/superhero movies. When she can find a snippet of free time, she is likely to be found reading, painting with watercolors, or enjoying nature. | @hmayophoto

HEIDI EITREIM is currently a stay-at-home homeschool mom in her fifth year. She has a BA in art with an emphasis in graphic design and recently reignited her passion for drawing and illustrating when she started teaching her children how to keep a nature journal. | @withheidijoy

JENNIFER DEES and her husband live in Long Beach, California. She homeschools her four children using the Charlotte Mason philosophy of education. She also makes oil paintings in her spare time. | @jendydees

KATIE OKANSKI lives with her family on the Canadian Shield, surrounded by clear lakes and red pines, where she is learning to live slowly and mindfully. She is a storytelling photographer, who loves to use her camera to frame the little things and the little people who bring her joy.

KATRIEN VAN DEUREN grew up in Belgium and moved to Northern Italy when she met her husband, Francesco. Now almost ten years later, they have five-year-old twin boys and a baby and make a conscious effort to build a slow, mindful life for themselves in close contact with nature. | @growingwildthings

KRISTIN ROGERS loves to laugh, learn, make fun of herself, let her children climb on her, and join them in their home-made forts. Her heart does a "pitter-patter" for nature, adoption, reading, coffee, homeschooling, thrift shops, messy hair, and tattoos. | @kristinrogers

MANDY LACKEY and her husband, Jeromy, live and play in North Texas with their two children. Mandy worked in the environmental science field before homeschooling. She loves how home education exposes every member of the family to wonderful literature and discoveries. | @mandybethlackey

MOGLI LOFTUS is wife to her best friend, and mama of two. She currently calls a historic fishing cottage in Iowa her home. Her background as a wildlife biologist and her life as an avid reader have been the major influences on her home education approach, and you can typically find her foraging, experimenting in the kitchen, concocting homemade remedies, or reading to her babies.

NAOMI OVANDO lives with her husband and children in sunny Southern California, where she homeschools her two boys and little girl. She is a hobbyist photographer and loves taking storytelling photos of her family and going on outdoor adventures. | @3bebesmama

NICHOLE HOLZE is an Iowa native now living in the South, happy to claim Arkansas as home. Mama to two incredible adventurers, she is a fearless wanderlust-and-coffee-fueled road tripper who has been known to take off for epic adventures at a moment's notice. | @coleyraeh

RACHAEL ALSBURY is an Enneagram type 5 who loves reading nonfiction, organizing things, and growing rosemary. On a regular day, you can find her at home in moccasins and a linen apron reading to her girls and playing in their front yard garden. Together they are finding joy and freedom in this season of learning at home. | @rachael.alsbury

RENEE HUSTON is a mother, teacher, and chai latte drinker. She recently moved from the suburbs of DC to a nineteenth-century farmhouse with her husband and three kids. She loves being surrounded by nature and her neighbor's fifty-acre sheep farm. As a former public school teacher, Renee enjoys using her love for teaching to homeschool her own kids. | @rmhuston

SUZI KERN lives in the mountains of East Tennessee with her three children and sleepy old lap dog. She is a regular contributor to the Wild + Free content bundles. | @suziqzikern

TIFFANY GRIFFIN is a homeschool mama of three Earth-side babes and one sweet girl who travels among the stars. She is a lifestyle photographer and visual storyteller with a deep love for capturing beauty in everyday moments. She also loves poetry, all things nature, art, and the thing that always feels like Christmas: thrifting.

ABOUT
WILD + FREE

Wild + Free is a community of families who believe children not only should receive a quality education but also are meant to experience the adventure, freedom, and wonder of childhood. Wild + Free exists to equip families with resources to raise and educate children at home, as well as to encourage and inspire them along the way.

To learn more about Wild + Free and join the community,
visit bewildandfree.org. | @wildandfree.co

CREDITS

Photographs of Wandering Close to Home on pages 2–5 by Hannah Mayo. Used with permission. Photographs of Foraging in Nature on pages 6–8 by Kristin Rogers. Used with permission. Photographs of The Lost Art of the Family Walk on pages 10–13 by Kristin Rogers. Used with permission. Photographs of Savoring Winter on pages 14–17 by Alisha Miller. Used with permission. Photographs of Growing into a Nature Mama on pages 18–21 by Bekah Maka. Used with permission. Photographs of Nature Journaling the Museum on pages 24–27 by Kristin Rogers. Used with permission. Photographs of Painting with Nature on pages 28–30 by Rachael Alsbury. Used with permission. Photographs of Nature Journaling Squirrels on pages 31–33 by Heidi Eitreim. Used with permission. Photographs of Plein Air Painting with Kids on pages 35–37 by Kristin Rogers. Used with permission. Photographs of Wildflower Adventures on pages 38–41 by Kristin Rogers. Used with permission. Photographs of Nurturing Outdoor Play (with a Mud Kitchen) on pages 44–46 by Rachael Alsbury. Used with permission. Photographs of Cultivating Patience (and Mushrooms) on page 48 by Suzi Kern and on pages 51–52 by Kristin Rogers. Used with permission. Photographs of Keeping Chickens on pages 54–58 by Kristin Rogers. Used with permission. Photographs of Nurturing Slow in the City on pages 59–61 by Kristin Rogers. Used with permission. Photographs of Edible Flower and Herb Cookies on pages 62–67 by Naomi Ovando. Used with permission. Photographs of The Naturalist at Home on pages 70 and 72 by Kristin Rogers and on page 73 by Jennifer Dees. Used with permission. Photographs of A Kitchen Scrap Garden on pages 74–79 by Mogli Loftus. Used with permission. Photographs of Creating a Backyard Haven on pages 80–84 by Tiffany Griffin. Used with permission. Photographs of Heirloom Seed Exchange on pages 85–88 by Suzi Kern. Used with permission. Photographs of Foraging Dandelions in Your Backyard on pages 89–93 by Mogli Loftus.

Used with permission. Photographs of Nature Study in the City on pages 96 and 99 by Kristin Rogers and on page 100 by Tiffany Griffin. Used with permission. Photographs of Exploring the National Parks on pages 101–104 by Naomi Ovando. Used with permission. Photographs of The Magic of Field Trips on pages 105–108 by Suzi Kern. Used with permission. Photographs of Camping for Beginners on page 109 by Mandy Lackey, on page 111 by Naomi Ovando, and on page 112 by Tiffany Griffin. Used with permission. Photographs of Forest Games on pages 113–117 by Rachael Alsbury. Used with permission.

Additional photography credits:

Page i: Kristin Rogers
Pages ii–iii, vi–vii: Rachael Alsbury
Pages iv–v: Naomi Ovando
Page viii: Katie Okanski
Pages x–xi: Kristin Rogers
Pages xii–1, 94–95: Katrien Van Deuren
Pages 22–23: Jennifer Dees
Pages 42–43: Hannah Mayo
Pages 68–69: Mandy Lackey
Page 118: Katie Okanski
Pages 119–123: Photographs courtesy of each contributor
Page 124: Rachel Kovac

Illustrations:

Recurring trees: pikolorante/Shutterstock
Page 4: Marsala Digital 2/Creative Market
Pages 7, 19, 30: Graphic Box/Creative Market
Page 9: Cutest art/Creative Market
Page 12: Ermakova Marina/Shutterstock
Pages 15, 16, 39, 64, 71, 92: Maria B. Paints/Creative Market
Page 25: Scarlet Heath Art/Creative Market
Pages 34, 49, 61, 81: Dainty Doll Art/Creative Market
Pages 46, 53: Mariart_i/Shutterstock
Page 51: dzujen/Shutterstock
Page 58: YesFoxy/Creative Market
Page 63: Julia M. Watercolor/Creative Market
Page 66: GraphicsDish/Creative Market
Page 76: Oaurea/Shutterstock
Pages 84, 117: tofutyklein/Shutterstock
Page 88: Sunny Illustrations/Creative Market
Pages 97, 110: lhorevna/Shutterstock
Page 98: Lembrik's Artworks/Creative Market
Page 107: Paulaparaula/Creative Market

Looking for more great activities to do with your kids?

Check out these other Wild + Free books full of crafts, activities, games, and more!

MAY 2021

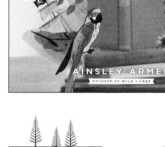